MW01165383

The Schoolhouse of Quality®

How *One Voice* Built A Better School

The Schoolhouse of Quality®

How *One Voice* Built A Better School

Gerald S. Hammond, FAIA
Stephen H. Schwandner, II

Foreword by David T. Kearns
Former Chairman and CEO of Xerox Corporation
and former U.S. Deputy Secretary of Education

The McGraw-Hill Companies, Inc.
College Custom Series

New York St. Louis San Francisco Auckland Bogotá
Caracas Lisbon London Madrid Mexico Milan Montreal
New Delhi Paris San Juan Singapore Sydney Tokyo Toronto

The Schoolhouse of Quality
How *One Voice* Built A Better School

The Schoolhouse of Quality is a registered servicemark
of Steed Hammond Paul Inc.

1 2 3 4 5 6 7 8 9 0 DOC.DOC 9 0 9 8 7 6

ISBN 0-07-057270-4

Editor: Jan Scipio
Cover Design: Jim Folzenlogen and Gerry Pasqualetti
Printer/Binder: R.R. Donnelley & Sons Company, Inc.

More Advance Praise for *The Schoolhouse of Quality*

"The Schoolhouse of Quality raises the bar and sets a new standard for community involvement in schools."

John Brunner
Director of Community Relations
Fairfield City School District

"We're believers in the process. It helped us pull together the diverse opinions of people throughout our school district, which serves the largest geographical area in Ohio."

Chris Armstrong
School Board Vice President
Adams County/Ohio Valley Local School District

"This is a paradigm-shifting book for those in the construction industry. Yes, we actually do have customers, and we must do a better job of involving them in our projects."

Mark McCollough
Vice President
Lionmark Construction Companies

"An important reminder to all education leaders that often the best thing we can do is listen. This book illustrates how to listen in a creative and effective way. "

Candace Koch
School Board Member
Batavia Local School District

"The Schoolhouse of Quality is a wonderful illustration of a very important concept for all businesses and organizations: focus on your customers or cease to exist."

Tim Schigel
President
Schigel & Associates
Customer-Driven Strategic Planning

Dedication

We dedicate this book to all those, whether in the private or public sector, who are committed to the noble and never-ending pursuit of Quality as it is defined by their Customers.

Table of Contents

Foreword

Much has been written about what lessons business can teach education. Having served as chairman and CEO of Xerox Corporation and later as U.S. Deputy Secretary of Education, I have concluded that one must be careful about drawing parallels between the two worlds. Yet there is at least one undeniable similarity between these two great institutions: meaningful, fundamental change does not come easy to either, nor can it come completely from within.

No rational person can examine the evidence and deny that our schools need changing. It's not, as some would have us believe, that there's absolutely nothing right with American education today. The bottom line is simply that our students aren't learning what they need for our country to stay competitive in the global market-place. The situation only worsens as both technology and the quality of education in other countries race ahead. The scope of the change needed is daunting and the urgency nothing short of immediate.

Managing the process of such change is never easy. Shortly after becoming chairman of Xerox in 1982, I was certain that if we did not undergo fundamental change, we would go out of business. Being at the helm while one of America's most respected and successful companies nose-dived into oblivion frightened me and the thousands of employees of Xerox into action.

The details of how Xerox employees turned the situation around can be found in *Prophets in the Dark*, a book I co-authored with David A. Nadler. However, at the core of the problem — and the key to solving it — was the fact that Xerox couldn't change on its own. It needed an outside perspective; it needed to hear the voice of its customers.

At Xerox we had, in essence, decided that we would tell our customers what they wanted and needed. We had developed the bad habit of ignoring our customers, while our Japanese competitors cozied up to them. While Xerox created unwanted products, our competitors offered solutions that fulfilled real needs and exceeded expectations. To make matters worse, we were building equipment at the same cost the Japanese were selling theirs! It didn't take a rocket scientist to see that this was a recipe for going out of business.

The situation began to turn around for Xerox only when we committed ourselves to truly listening to our customers — both internal and external. No longer were we defining quality for them, they began defining it for us. This customer-focused approach has brought Xerox back from the edge of the precipice and returned it to a place of international success and respect.

American education must undergo similar fundamental change if the reforms we so desperately need are to become reality. And this change simply cannot happen without the perspective and participation from those out-

side the system. The voices heard must not only be those
of administrators and teachers, but parents, students, business leaders and the community at large. Just as quality
couldn't be defined and achieved solely by a group of
Xerox product engineers, neither can educational quality
be defined and achieved by a group of educators working
in a vacuum.

This is not to imply that Xerox doesn't need product
engineers or that education reform doesn't require professional educators. To the contrary, the importance and
necessity of their roles only increase with customer participation. After all, no quality process is in itself a
panacea or a silver bullet. At Xerox, the customer and
market feedback would mean nothing if we couldn't at
the end of the day build better copiers.

At Xerox, senior managers are required to spend one
day a month answering customers' calls. Listening to customers who were disappointed in our products and services was painful, but it did give us much needed intelli-
gence. It's not as if we made radical changes based on
every single comment from every customer. Rather, we
blended the voices together to find common themes and
establish priorities.

When those concerned about education do the same
thing, they too will find themselves in the position of hearing things that they'd rather not. But it will soon become
clear, as it became clear to Xerox, that in all those voices
are some answers to the toughest challenges we face.

Applying this process to education is no easy matter.
For example, how does one set about building consensus

around difficult and sometimes volatile issues like year-round schooling and academic standards? It requires a precise process for finding harmony among many diverse and sometimes competing voices.

In this book, One Voice explains just such a process. Created by Steed Hammond Paul, The Schoolhouse of Quality represents an innovative means of applying private-sector quality initiatives to education. While the focus of this story is building better schoolhouses where better learning and teaching can take place, the fundamentals of The Schoolhouse of Quality can be applied to any education process.

We will never reform education until we do a better job of building consensus and support for the difficult issues we face. One Voice shows us a great way to get started.

You're reading this book because you care deeply about our schools and our children's future. I salute you and say: Apply what you learn from the story of One Voice to your unique situation and let your voice be heard. But when you're done, make time and listen to other voices. Together, your voices will do great things for education.

David T. Kearns
November 1996

The Schoolhouse of Quality®

How *One Voice* Built A Better School

Chapter 1

ONE VOICE SPEAKS UP

The Architect was in trouble midway through the presentation, and knew it. The room was full and everyone was most attentive, but the atmosphere lacked the energy that sweeps the audience when a great presentation is reaching its crescendo. Stepping away from the easel that held the color rendering of the new school building, he collapsed his pointer and returned it to his pocket. "Ladies and gentlemen, there you have it. I'm sure you will agree we have produced a compelling design for your new school."

Several seconds of awkward silence followed. To The Architect, it seemed an eternity.

Finally, The Voice of the School Board President was heard. "Ahem. Thank you very much for your presentation. It's obvious your firm logged a lot of hours on this project, and we're very appreciative. Does anyone have a question or comment?"

Silence again.

Then, a hand raised at the back of the room. Another voice was heard. It was The Voice of the Taxpayer. "If you ask me, it's way too lavish. When I was a child, we made do with a room, a book, a chair and a teacher. What you have here will cost way too much."

Another hand. Another voice. This time, The Voice of the Teacher. "Things have changed since you were a child. Our children's needs are much different today. I like the exterior design, but the classrooms are all wrong. If someone had just talked to me about how I conduct my classes..."

Before The Voice of the Teacher could finish, another voice was heard. It was The Voice of the Parent. "I just want to feel sure that this is going to be the best design for my child's education. That's my only concern. These kids are our future."

The Voice of the Coach grumbled, "I can see the athletic program was last in line when you started doling out the dollars."

The Voice of the Superintendent attempted to reply. "We used a very classical approach to developing the priorities given to the designers..."

"Classical according to who?" shouted The Voice of the Music Director in the direction of the Coach. "Athletics got a whole lot more out of this design than we did."

"Uh, hello," said The Voice of the Student, sarcastically. "Does anybody care what the students think? Or is this all just a big game?"

"Too much money."

"Not enough space."

"I don't like the way it looks."

"Too much emphasis on this program."

"Not enough emphasis on that program."

"It's unfair!"

"No, it's not."

"Yes, it is!"

The Architect was perspiring. The meeting was out of control. The Voice of the School Board President could barely be heard above the clamor. "Order! Order! We will have order! Please, ladies and gentlemen." The noise subsided.

A hand had been raised throughout the entire, wild exchange. "Yes," said The Voice of the School Board President, "you have the floor. You may proceed."

One Voice spoke up. "We ought to be approaching this the way we do things at my company."

"And just what company do you own?" The Voice of the Business Leader asked wryly.

"Oh, I didn't say I owned a company," said One Voice. "But I do own part of a process. We don't have a design problem here. We have a Quality process problem."

"I told you we had a Quality problem," The Voice of the Teacher said. "I told you the classrooms were all wrong. I knew it."

"Now, wait a minute," said One Voice. "I didn't say we had a Quality problem. I said we had a Quality process problem."

"And just what do you mean when you say you own part of a process?" asked The Voice of the Business Leader.

"May I?" asked One Voice.

"Please, ladies and gentlemen," said The Voice of the School Board President. "Give the speaker your attention."

"Thank you," said One Voice. "No doubt many of you are familiar with the company where I work. In fact, some of my co-workers are here tonight. Our company has employed a lot of people in this community over the years, but as you know, a few years ago we nearly went belly-up.

"Anyway, this motivated our CEO to start thinking differently," One Voice continued. "The day after the Thanksgiving break, he called us all together and told us how we had forgotten how to listen. Nonsense, we thought. We'd been listening to every direction and change of direction that management had been making for 20 years. Someone called the boss on it. Yeah, right there, one of my co-workers shouted out, 'Who you sayin' we're not listening to?' And that's when the CEO pinned it on us really good."

"What was the answer?" asked The Voice of the Business Leader.

"The Customer," said One Voice. "The CEO told us we had forgotten how to listen to The Voice of the Customer. The CEO was right. The fact is, I hadn't seen, spoken or listened to a real customer since I went to work at the company. In the truest sense, I don't think we had forgotten how to listen to The Voice of the Customer. Most of us had never done it to begin with.

"What we've learned these last few years," said One Voice, "is that 'Quality' begins and ends in the mind of The Customer. Our CEO made the pursuit of customer-defined Quality our company's number one priority. Our entire workflow has been rearranged such that each of us feels a definite connection to The Customer. Each of us 'owns' a part of the process that ultimately delivers on The Customers' expectations. We understand better than ever what real Quality means."

"Oh, this is just all that Japanese TQM mumbo-jumbo," scolded The Voice of the Taxpayer. "We Americans are still the mightiest, most productive workforce on the planet. I've never driven a foreign-made automobile, and I never will. We don't need to be taking our cues from any..."

"It's true," said One Voice. "The 'Quality' movement did originate in post-World War II Japan. People like Dr. W. Edwards Deming and Dr. Joseph Juran helped the Japanese rebuild their economy by introducing this customer-driven focus into their work processes. But many American companies have now embraced customer-focused processes as the way to deliver world-class goods and services. And it's not just automakers and other manufacturers. Banks are using this approach. So are hotels and all kinds of service businesses. Some believe that as the Quality movement made its way through America in the last 20 years, the whole art of delivering customer-defined Quality has been elevated to a new level here in the United States."

"Things are certainly booming out at your company now," said The Voice of the Business Leader, enviously. "Your CEO must be doing something right."

"It's not just our CEO," said One Voice. "We're all doing something right. In fact, we've all made a commitment to doing everything right the first time. That's part of what I meant when I said I own a process. I'm responsible for seeing that my part of the process is consistently delivering on The Customers' expectations."

"Pardon me if I don't see one bit of relevance in all this," said The Voice of the Taxpayer. "Did we come here to listen to a speech about this person's company, or are we going to get on with voting to reject this preposterous school building design?"

"But, it is relevant," said One Voice. "This is the third time this architect has been to this school board to present a design."

The Architect grimaced and nodded nervously.

"If the process had been different, if it had truly been driven by The Voice of the Customer, The Architect would have been able to get it right the first time," said One Voice.

The Voice of the Superintendent responded gruffly, "I can tell you that I have spent many long hours with this design firm. I have worked tirelessly to see that they could proceed with the most comprehensive set of directions I could possibly give them."

"Oh, please, I didn't mean to offend you," said One Voice. "I didn't mean to suggest that you had done anything other than your very best to facilitate this project. But frankly, you are only one of many customers."

"Well, it is my responsibility," said The Voice of the Superintendent.

"Indeed it is," said One Voice, "but you're not the only Customer."

"Yeah," shouted The Voice of the Student, "I'm the customer! It's the students you ought be listening to."

"And I suppose that you plan to foot the bill for this school building?" asked The Voice of the Taxpayer. "No, young one, 'They who have the gold make the rules.' I'm The Customer."

"I'm the one you're expecting to deliver the results," said The Voice of the Teacher. "I think I'm The Customer."

"No, I'm the one expecting the results," said The Voice of the Parent. "I'm The Customer."

"You're the one expecting the results?!" replied The Voice of the Business Leader. "I'm the one who is depending on this school system to provide me with capable and skilled workers. I think I'm The Customer."

"I am!"

"No, I am!"

"No, I am!"

"Ladies and gentlemen, please!" shouted The Voice of the School Board President as the meeting was gaveled back to order. "Well," he said to One Voice, "as you can see, your company's management approach doesn't quite work here. This is a school system, not a business."

"Let's get on with the vote!" shouted The Voice of the Taxpayer.

One Voice was still standing.

"Is there something else you would like to add?" asked The Voice of the School Board President.

"We can design this school building the way we design and deliver products and services at my company," pleaded One Voice. "We can build The Schoolhouse of Quality. I am sure of it."

"What makes you so sure?" asked The Voice of the School Board President.

"Because I know who The Customer is," replied One Voice.

"Oohs" and "ahs" resounded throughout the room. The atmosphere was suddenly charged like the dramatic moment when Perry Mason turns from the witness stand to point an accusing finger at a frantic courtroom observer.

"Well," asked The Voice of the School Board President, "who is it?"

"The Customer is us," One Voice said simply. "It's all of us."

"Well, just how do you propose to satisfy all of us?" asked The Voice of the Coach. "I won't be satisfied until I get a bigger piece of the pie for my program..."

"You already have too big a piece," cried The Voice of the Music Teacher.

"We can develop a design that everyone finds satisfactory," answered One Voice. "We can do it the same way we reconcile all the different needs and desires that my company's customers have. The tools and techniques exist to build a consensus about customer-defined Quality among large, diverse groups of customers. We could use those same private sector and market process tools to design this building."

"Yes!" shouted The Voice of the Parent. "You're talking about brainstorming. We did something like that at a PTA meeting last year and..."

"No, I'm talking about something more than brainstorming," said One Voice. "In brainstorming, you collect a lot of interesting ideas, and there are occasional creative breakthroughs, but the results are too often impractical, unattainable and pie-in-the-sky. We need to utilize techniques that are far more objective than brainstorming."

"Right!" said The Voice of the Business Leader. "We need to do some research. We'll select a scientifically reliable group at random and we'll survey them to find out the kind of building they want."

"Not quite," said One Voice. "We will have to do some surveying, but the kind of information we'll collect will be different from most surveys. It'll be the kind of input that a design team needs to develop the innovative solutions that satisfy The Customer. There will need to be some live participation on the part of many people for us to succeed in building The Schoolhouse of Quality."

"Don't you call those meetings 'focus groups'?" asked The Voice of the Teacher. "I remember participating in a focus group for a textbook publisher one time. It was very interesting."

"At the beginning of our process, we will use some techniques that look like focus groups," said One Voice. "After those group sessions are completed, we'll broaden our research effort to be sure we get solid, reliable results."

"A town meeting! Now you're talking," exclaimed The Voice of the Taxpayer. "There isn't anything we can't accomplish by getting free men and women into one room and letting them debate the pros and cons."

"Our approach will be very democratic," said One Voice. "But it won't really be a town meeting. Town meetings are too often dominated by a few loud and assertive people."

There were a few snickers. The Taxpayer folded his arms, frowned and slid back into his chair.

The Architect had been silent through all of this. Now he spoke, his voice quivering with a degree of sarcasm and indignation. "I suppose that I can just go on home, now. It doesn't sound as if you'll need an architect to design your building. If you follow this person's recommendation, it sounds like you'll be able to just design it yourself. We in the architectural profession like to think we've learned a thing or two about designing buildings, but maybe with these new, modern techniques you won't need us." The Architect packed the rendering into his portfolio and got up to leave the room.

Ouch! The crowd watched nervously to see how One Voice would handle The Architect's parting shot.

"Oh, wait, you can't leave," pleaded One Voice. "We need you, because we don't know the technical aspects of designing a building. We can play a role in coming up with some ideas for meeting The Customers' needs. But you have to work with us to ultimately design the building. We wouldn't even know where to start. You and your colleagues are the ones who will bring that experience to this process. You're a vital part of our team."

The Architect was reassured, and a bit embarrassed about the way he reacted.

"Can't we just vote this design down, and go home?" asked The Voice of the Taxpayer.

A buzz of conversation moved across the room. The Voice of the Parent spoke up.

"I think we should give One Voice's idea a chance."

"I agree," said The Voice of the Teacher.

"Oh, for goodness' sake!" cried The Voice of the Taxpayer. "This is just going to cost us more time and more money. Am I the only one here who has any respect for the hard-earned dollar?"

"If we do this right the first time," answered One Voice, "we can build this school better, faster and less expensively. We've already been through some considerable expense on three rounds of designs, and we're no closer to a school building."

"It's getting late," said The Voice of the School Board President. "May I suggest that One Voice spend some time with The Architect? Perhaps together they can arrive at an approach that will help us through this impasse."

The Architect was reticent to yield any control to One Voice, but it was apparent that to do anything else was to put the project on ice. "I am sure that my colleagues at our firm would find One Voice's ideas very interesting," he said grudgingly.

"I am happy to help in any way that I can," said One Voice.

Chapter 2

BACK TO THE DRAWING BOARD

Tymeliss, Frugill, Eeger & Arteest was arguably the most experienced school architectural firm in the state. In fact, it was TFE&A's specialization in school buildings that had attracted The Architect to the firm right out of college. During seven years with the practice, The Architect had been tutored by the firm's very experienced, yet very different partners.

Were a Hollywood producer to call Central Casting in search of an architect archetype, Tymeliss would fill the bill. Every hair on his silver-maned head was combed to mimic that of Frank Lloyd Wright, whose portrait was prominently displayed above his desk.

Frugill was the firm's left brain. It was said that he could mentally erect an entire building starting with just one ten-penny nail, then disassemble it just as easily. Client dollars were treated as if they were Frugill's own, and the clutch of his fist was not easily loosened. Respect for budgets was a cornerstone of TFE&A's fine reputation in the educational community.

Eeger began professional life as an architect, but somewhere along the way had been transformed into an entrepreneur. To Eeger, TFE&A was not the classical "practice" of professionals, but rather an enterprise that was always lurching toward new, undiscovered horizons. Eeger was a paradoxical character who on the one hand championed the heritage of the profession, but on the other was intent on making TFE&A into something new. This was Eeger's form of creative expression.

Arteest's expression, conversely, knew no form. In Arteest resided the firm's raw creative spirit. Many times Arteest's hubris had collided head-on with the cold rationality of Frugill's spreadsheets and estimates. When Arteest and Frugill set sparks flying, the wisdom of Tymeliss and the aspirations of Eeger would always provide just the right counterbalances. TFE&A's clients were the beneficiaries of the greater whole that emerged from the sum of these parts.

What a great environment this had been for The Architect to launch and develop a career. All of the senior partners were wonderful teachers in their own right. Each had placed tremendous confidence in The Architect. The last thing he ever wanted to do was disappoint them. But as he made his way into the firm's conference room to brief the partners on the status of his project, he was afraid that disappointing them was exactly what he was about to do.

"Come in, come in," said Tymeliss. "We've been waiting for you. We're sure the plans were well received by the school board this time. Weren't they?" The volume and enthusiasm of Tymeliss's voice softened in the presence of the anguished look on The Architect's face.

"Oh, don't tell me we're going to have do this thing over again!" said Frugill. "Do you know how many hours we've put into this project already?"

"Face it," said Arteest. "Those people wouldn't know good design if it smacked them in the face. Just give me your notes on the feedback from the meeting and we'll churn out another set of drawings."

"I'm afraid it won't be that easy," said The Architect. "They not only want us to do something different, they want us to do it differently."

"I don't understand," said Tymeliss.

The Architect proceeded to recount the events of the previous evening's school board meeting, and did as best he could to explain the approach that One Voice suggested they take to designing the school.

"Why, that's design-by-committee," scoffed Arteest.

"I thought so, too," responded The Architect. "But they're calling it a 'Quality' approach to design. I don't know much about it, but it sounds like something I'm going to have to learn."

"We're architects, for goodness' sake!" cried Frugill. "We're not marketing researchers or dishwasher designers. We build schools."

"One Voice says you could design schools using a 'Quality' approach," replied The Architect.

"And you can."

None of the architects knew just how long One Voice had been eavesdropping on their debate. With a tone of discomfort and embarrassment, The Architect said, "Oh, thank you very much for coming today. May I introduce you to our firm's namesakes, Tymeliss, Frugill, Eeger and Arteest? Everyone, would you please welcome One Voice?"

One Voice exchanged greetings with each of the architects, then took a seat at the table. "Excuse me for being a few minutes early."

"No problem," offered Tymeliss as he simultaneously gave The Architect a reproving glare for the surprise appearance of their meeting's guest. The Architect shifted in his chair. If only he had gained the advantage of a few more minutes to prepare his superiors for One Voice's participation.

"We are certainly glad to have you with us, One Voice," said Tymeliss, "though we must confess we're not exactly sure of your purpose."

"Well, The Architect asked me to come over today to tell you about how we might use Total Quality Management principles to design our new school building."

"Fine. Well, please tell us," said Frugill while glancing at the time on the clock. "I may have to excuse myself shortly to get back on these drawings. We do have a school building to build, don't we?"

"You need to build consensus before you build anything else," said One Voice.

"We are accustomed to building things that are, shall we say, more 'structural,'" said Tymeliss. "Could you elaborate?"

"Quality is in the mind of The Customer," said One Voice. "For years, we thought Quality was in the hands of the supplier, but it is really the other way around. To build The Schoolhouse of Quality, we're going to have to listen intently to The Voice of the Customer."

"This firm has been serving customers, or clients as we call them, for more than 50 years. We know how to take care of customers," said Tymeliss.

"Um, excuse me, Boss," said The Architect, tentatively, "but One Voice says that all of the voices we're hearing at these school board meetings – teachers, parents, students, taxpayers, coaches – all of them combine to represent The Voice of the School Building Customer."

"I thought I taught you better," said Tymeliss. "This still appears to be nothing more than design-by-committee, a practice we abhor with good reason."

"I don't think that's what he's talking about," said Eeger. "I've read a few things recently about companies that have embraced TQM and other customer-driven business practices. This stuff is different than what we've always regarded as design-by-committee."

"Then let's permit One Voice to explain the difference," said Tymeliss. "Where do we begin?"

"You begin by asking different kinds of questions," said One Voice.

"Like what?" asked Arteest.

"What kinds of questions do you ask now, as you begin a project?" replied One Voice.

"Typical things. 'How many students do you have? What kind of enrollment growth are you anticipating, if any? How many seats do want in the auditorium? How many new classrooms?' Those kinds of questions," replied Arteest.

"Did you ever think to ask them about their values?" suggested One Voice.

"You mean like their religious or personal philosophies?" asked Arteest.

"Perhaps not quite that esoteric. In the case of the school building we're working on now, have you asked anything like, 'What qualities would have to be reflected in the facility to foster world-class education?'"

"Sure we have," said Frugill. "They said they wanted things like an easier-to-maintain roof, wider hallways, and better lighting in the classroom."

"No," said One Voice. "I'm talking about 10,000-feet types of questions. You're flying down here with 1,000-feet types of issues." One Voice's hand moved through the air like a dive-bombing fighter plane.

"I'm confused," said Tymeliss. "You must be patient with us, One Voice. When you speak of 10,000 feet, I'm afraid we take those concepts only too literally."

"Okay," said One Voice. "Customers don't buy easily maintained roofs, they buy comfort from the elements. They don't buy wide hallways, they buy ease of mobility through the buildings. They don't buy better lighting, t ey buy an environment in which they are more confident that students will have a better chance of learning. Don't you see the difference?" asked One Voice.

"It's classical features and benefits from Marketing 101," said Eeger. "You sell benefits and deliver features."

"That's somewhat true," said One Voice. "Only I think we're really talking about focusing on the benefits. Features are important. However, how the features deliver on The Customer's expectation of perceived benefits is, in the end, the essence of Quality."

"Okay, so you gather lots of input from people representing all of the various user groups in the school district. Then what?" asked Eeger.

"Then you assemble a few people who represent each user group, plus professionals from your staff, and maybe some outside experts, and you call this whole new group the Community Design Team. The Team takes the values identified by the research and uses them to develop Design Concepts that will deliver on the expectations of The Customer," replied One Voice.

"There's your committee," said Tymeliss.

"It's really not a committee," said One Voice. "Even though the Community Design Team's efforts will be intensely spontaneous and creative, they will also be very structured. All of the Community Design Team's decisions and conclusions will be filtered through a very rational and objective design and planning model driven by The Customers' values. Similar processes have been used to design all kinds of products and services. In the end, it is very rational and tightly quantified."

"Looks like you won't need me. This Community Design Team of yours ought to be able to take it from there," Arteest said, with eyes rolling.

"The Architect said the same thing at the school board meeting," said One Voice. "Let me emphasize to all of you, this project needs you. The result of this process is a strategic map or, if you will, an 'architecture' of customer expectations. We will still depend on your creativity and expertise to help us refine those Design Concepts and deliver the building that satisfies those expectations."

"We are architects," said Tymeliss. "Our entire educa-tion and professional experience have prepared us to know what's best. We will not let that important role be assumed by a group of laypeople. We will not be clerks to some brainstorming exercise."

"You are indeed the authorities on how technically to deliver on the expectations," One Voice responded. "But The Customer is the authority on those expectations. All I am suggesting is that you do a more thorough job of submitting to that authority. I can assure you that as you do so, The Customer's respect for your authority will only be enhanced."

Frugill had heard enough. "Has anyone thought for a moment just how many more hours this is going to add to this project? This will take forever! This school district is out of room. They need a building now. We can't dicker around for another 90 days asking touchy-feely questions. We need to get to work!"

"I couldn't help but overhear your earlier complaint about how much time and effort has already been put into this project. Do you really think that diving headlong into another round of aimless exploration will gain the endorsement of this school board?" One Voice challenged. "Your approach has been plan-do, plan-do, plan-do. You're getting nowhere."

"So you're just going to slow down the whole process and cost us valuable time instead," said Frugill.

"No," said One Voice. "You propose another round of plan-do. I propose a new round of plaaaaaaaaaan-do." As the word "plan" was spoken, One Voice's hands extended to full reach as if a magnificent fish story was in the telling. "If you plaaaaaaaaan and do, in the end you will eliminate costly trial and error, and you will be more likely to deliver a product that satisfies."

Frugill wasn't convinced. "We've done a few school buildings in our time. If you open this thing up that wide, you're going to get a shopping list of wishes that we will never be able to satisfy. They won't be able to afford it. When we're done with your approach, there will be nothing but a lot of disappointed and angry people."

"It doesn't have to be that way," said One Voice. "People know their desires and people know their resources. Those ideas that can't be funded because of lack of resources won't be, but The Customers will make that decision for themselves through an objective process, rather than your making it for them. Anyway, supply often creates its own demand. Resources you may think don't exist, sometimes materialize when there is a truly good idea. I think you'll be surprised."

"Well, let me just saaaaaaaaay to you, One Voice, we need to get another set of drawings in front of this Customer", said Arteest. "I can have another set of drawings by next Friday."

The Architect winced. Now he had to come clean with the management team. "Look, we don't have any choice. We're either going to try to make it work this way or, frankly, the school board will go find a firm that is willing to take this approach."

"Now you really have my attention," said Eeger. "This is a big project, Tymeliss. We can't afford to just walk away from it."

The senior partner stroked his chin. "Indeed," is all he said.

The Architect spoke. "Look, I'm beginning to get comfortable with this approach. Let me run with it. I'm sure One Voice will help."

One Voice smiled and nodded.

"I'm interested, too," said Eeger. "I think this could be some fascinating new ground for us to cover."

Frugill glanced at Arteest. For once, they were in agreement. Arteest rose from the table and said, "After you have finished all of your emotional encounter groups, let us know. Then Frugill and I will get back to the job of designing a school."

Chapter 3

BEFORE YOU BUILD ANYTHING ELSE, BUILD A HOUSE

The Architect had become a believer.

During the last three weeks, instead of working on another design presentation, The Architect had spent his time learning everything he could about Total Quality Management and the specific techniques that One Voice's company had used to effect its dramatic turnaround. While there was still much to learn, The Architect now understood better than ever how the approach One Voice championed could be used to break through the school building impasse.

Now representatives of the school's "stakeholders" were assembled for a follow-up public meeting to discuss the next steps in the new design process. "World-class companies use this process to deliver high-quality goods and services," The Architect began, "and today we're going to show you how we're going to use the same process to deliver a world-class school building."

The group watched curiously as The Architect unveiled the board on his presentation easel. This time, rather than an elaborate full-color rendering of a proposed new school building, the easel displayed a simple illustration of a small, two-dimensional planning chart.

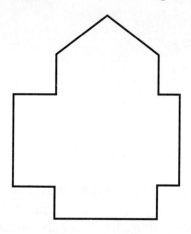

"We're going to build a house," said The Architect.

"A house!" sounded The Voice of the Coach. "Well, now we're really off the track. When are we going to get back to dealing with the issue of designing our school?"

"Relax, my friend," said The Architect. "I'm speaking figuratively. One Voice, perhaps you could help us understand this house by telling us something about the origin of the process."

"Gladly," said One Voice. "The design and planning process we're going to employ was actually first used in 1972 by Mitsubishi. It is an evolution of a management approach known as Quality Function Deployment, or

QFD, which has since been used by many world-class companies and organizations including Ford, Texas Instruments, Ritz Carlton, Xerox, NASA and Kodak.

"The house we're about to build refers to the shape of the strategic map we will be using to guide both our participants and professional designers to the delivery of a Quality finished school building. Those who use QFD call this strategic map the 'House of Quality.' For our purposes, we can just as easily call this diagram our 'Schoolhouse of Quality.'"

"I don't know," said The Voice of the Coach. "I'm still skeptical."

"Great!" said One Voice. "You've revealed one of truths of The Schoolhouse of Quality process." One Voice turned to the chalkboard at the front of the room and wrote these words:

You will be skeptical, but you will be convinced.

The Coach settled back into his chair with a look of puzzlement on his face.

"How is this going to help us get moving again on our school building?" asked The Voice of the Parent. "I'm confused."

"Before we answer that question," said One Voice, "let me just state that you've revealed yet another truth. One Voice returned to the board and wrote:

You will be confused, but you will experience clarity.

"Let me try to make things clearer to you now," said The Architect. "Before we present another drawing or recommendation on this project, we're going to get everyone under one roof. This roof," he said pointing to the top of Schoolhouse of Quality diagram. "You represent the foundation of this schoolhouse, then we build very strong walls and a very well engineered roof."

"The Schoolhouse of Quality begins with The Voice of the Customer," said One Voice. "As we've already discussed, in the case of a school building, The Customer is an assimilation of all of the various voices of the people who will be served by the school: parents, teachers, administrators, taxpayers, students, etc."

"Over the course of the next few weeks," said The Architect, "we'll be seeking input and feedback from a large number of customers in this school district. We'll start with various forms of Customer research, and then move to smaller Community Design Team sessions made up of people like you who have the time, willingness and interest to contribute to make sure we do this job right."

The Voice of the Superintendent spoke. "I hate to cover old ground, but isn't this just old-fashioned survey research?"

"Not really," said The Architect. "What we are trying to do with these initial phases of the process is to identify what we call Customer Values. These are phrases and expressions we will use to describe issues of importance to Customers about our new school."

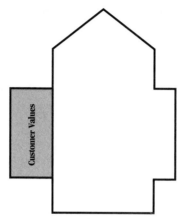

"For instance," The Architect continued, "automakers have used this process to identify the qualities Customers desire about a car door, such as it is 'easy to close' or 'stays open on an incline' or 'doesn't rattle and make noise.' We want to collect and assimilate as many of these kinds of expressions of Customer Values regarding our school building."

"Can't we just dive into it?" asked The Voice of the Superintendent. "I'm getting awfully impatient."

"Our problem is that we've been 'diving into it,' and that's part of why we're at an impasse," replied The Architect.

"Excuse me," said One Voice, "but I'd like to point out that you've uncovered another truth about our process:"

You will be impatient, but you will feel accomplishment.

The Architect continued. "After we collect these Customer Values, we will find out how important they really are. We will have Customers rate them on their importance and current performance." The Architect walked back to the easel and pointed to the right side of the schoolhouse diagram.

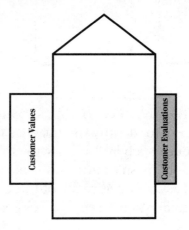

"Then we'll help you recruit a Community Design Team of representatives from each of our customer groups and several design professionals from my firm," said The Architect. "This group will collaborate to turn the values expressed by the Customers into concrete ideas for the new building. We call these ideas Design Concepts."

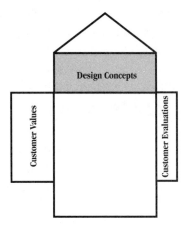

"With all due respect," said The Voice of the Business Leader, "most of these people have never had any experience with this kind of thing. Shouldn't we limit the design team to those who have actually been involved in construction?"

"Absolutely not," said One Voice. "The high-quality school building we're about to design will be the product of collaboration between people who have experience in constructing school buildings and others who have even more experience in using school buildings."

"Yes, but I challenge anyone here, other than perhaps The Architect, to come up with ideas more workable than my own. I'll have you know I've personally overseen the construction of more than a dozen buildings of this scale. I know a thing or two about construction," The Voice of the Business Leader reiterated.

"And that's exactly why we want you involved," said The Architect. "We're glad you've laid down the challenge to the other members of the group, but you should be

prepared to be challenged as well." The Architect nodded in the direction of One Voice, who returned to the
chalkboard.

You will be challenged, but you will see good ideas prevail.

"Next, we get down to the really hard part of this
process, and that's trying to reconcile and prioritize these
Customer Values and Design Concepts," said The
Architect.

"How does that happen?" asked The Voice of the
Superintendent.

"Our Community Design Team will work through
every brick in this schoolhouse where Customer Values
intersect with Design Concepts. We will force ourselves
to arrive at a consensus as to how well each Design
Concept along with its Target delivers on each Customer
Value. Finally, we will determine the importance of each
of these Concepts."

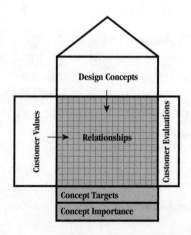

"Every single box on that chart!" said The Voice of the Teacher. "That has to be an incredibly long meeting. Right now your chart is a simple illustration, but I bet once we actually start designing a real school building, it's going to get a lot larger and more complex. Why, we'll be exhausted by the time we get through it all."

"The schoolhouse map will, in fact, be much larger and much more complex," answered The Architect. "But believe me, we can work through this. It will be an effort that requires a lot of physical and emotional stamina on the part of us all. In fact, that's another one of the truths of this process." The Architect took a turn at the board.

You will be tired, but you will end up invigorated.

"Finally, as I mentioned earlier, the architects will add their professional value to complete the process," The Architect explained. "With your help, we will have created a very objective road map that will guide our designers' efforts in coming up with workable solutions for this school district. It's not that the architects' creativity will be hindered or inhibited, but rather channeled properly. Every suggestion or design solution they make will be evaluated in the context of the conceptual schoolhouse you've built, and every change or new idea you propose along the way will, likewise, be assessed against the objectivity of the map developed by the Community Design Team. This completed house illustrates our goal, a schoolhouse that satisfies the needs and expectations of our Customers."

The Voice of the Coach spoke. "Maybe I'm just stubborn, but I will tell you all at the very beginning that I have one interest and one interest only: my athletic program. That's the only thing I'm interested in, and it's the only reason I plan to be at the table."

"I'm so glad you made that point," said One Voice. "I was afraid I almost forgot the final truth of this approach.

"What's that?" asked The Voice of the Coach.

You will be stubborn, but you will have new respect for the opinions of others.

The School Board President had remained silent throughout this exchange. As the meeting appeared to be drawing to a close, The Voice of the School Board President was heard. "Excuse me, ladies and gentlemen, but before we proceed, I have some concerns I don't think we've considered."

"I'm sorry," said The Architect. "Is there something I've overlooked?"

"Well, it's not a bricks-and-mortar thing," said The Voice of the School Board President. "I mean, you have shown us a very thoughtful approach to building consensus around our new school building, and certainly this approach will take us to a place we've been unable to reach up to now. But even if we get there, I'm not sure we'll break through the impasse."

"Why not?" asked The Architect.

"Because we've stumbled over ourselves so many times on this project, we've lost a lot of credibility," The Voice of the School Board President lamented. "At this point, we could use your approach to design an eighth wonder of the world, but it wouldn't pass muster without our constituents' confidence. You've said we have to build consensus before we build anything, but it seems to me that building trust is our first challenge."

"And we will be building trust," said One Voice. "Keep in mind that as we start this process, we will, for the first time, be involving representatives of all the building's Customer groups in the decision-making process. Because we're incorporating their opinions, we will already be gaining their trust. But it's also possible to build trust as a separate goal from building a new school building. It's just a matter of building another house."

The group was puzzled.

"If this approach can help build automobiles, if this approach can help build schools, then this approach can also build trust," announced One Voice.

"Let me show you how."

Chapter 4

BUILDING TRUST

One Voice stood in front of a blank pad on the easel with marker in hand. "Let's pretend that you folks are parents who have children at our school, and we brought you together for a focus group discussion about building trust. And let's also assume that I am leading the focus group discussion. I would begin by asking, 'What would it take to build a high level of trust between the School Board and Superintendent of this school district and customers such as yourself?'"

One Voice waited for his role-playing focus group to answer. No one spoke up immediately.

"Okay, let me see if I can help you," said One Voice. "Our School Board President has told us that we're not going to move forward on this project because people don't trust us. Why don't they trust us? And what will it take to gain their trust?"

"The leadership can start by keeping their promises," said The Voice of the Parent. "They've made three announcements about a new school building and haven't lived up to one deadline yet."

"That's exactly the kind of thing we're looking for," said One Voice as the first item went up on the pad.

```
┌─────────────────────────────────────────┐
│                                         │
│        DELIVER ON PROMISES MADE          │
│                                         │
└─────────────────────────────────────────┘
```

"Does anyone else have a suggestion? Again, what would it take to build a high level of trust between the leaders of this school district and its parents?"

"I think they should demonstrate greater respect for my hard-earned dollar," said The Voice of the Taxpayer.

One Voice added the new suggestion to the list:

```
┌─────────────────────────────────────────┐
│                                         │
│        DELIVER ON PROMISES MADE          │
│                                         │
│     MANAGE TAX DOLLARS MORE EFFECTIVELY  │
│                                         │
└─────────────────────────────────────────┘
```

"Very good," said One Voice. "These expressions are Customer Values. They are the raw material from which we will shape Solutions aimed at building trust. Surely there are more."

The Parent's hand was raised. "Frankly, I don't think the leadership has shown enough respect for people's opinions. They can go out there seeking all this input and involvement, but unless the leadership is committed to showing genuine respect and consideration for these opinions, it won't make any difference."

The list was expanded.

DELIVER ON PROMISES MADE

MANAGE TAX DOLLARS MORE EFFECTIVELY

DEMONSTRATE RESPECT FOR OPINIONS OF OTHERS

"You've just got to keep people informed," said The Voice of the Teacher. "You wouldn't believe how much misinformation is out there about this building program. They're not doing a good job of getting the information out and, as a consequence, the rumormongers and naysayers are the ones who are doing the best job of influencing opinion. 'Keep people informed.' Write that up on your pad."

One Voice obliged.

DELIVER ON PROMISES MADE

MANAGE TAX DOLLARS MORE EFFECTIVELY

DEMONSTRATE RESPECT FOR OPINIONS OF OTHERS

KEEP PEOPLE INFORMED

"What would it take to build a high level of trust between the leaders of this school district and its parents?" One Voice asked again.

"You may not believe this," said The Voice of the Coach, "but we still have people in this community who don't understand just how much we need a new school. They're frozen back in time at a place when they went to school here. They think 'It was fine then and it should be fine now,' and they don't understand how this district has grown and changed in the last 20 years."

The others nodded in agreement.

The Coach valued the affirmation from the group. "You all know what I'm talking about here. If the leadership is ever going to get these people to trust them, they darn well better prove beyond a shadow of a doubt just how desperately we need a new building."

One Voice updated the list of Customer Values.

DELIVER ON PROMISES MADE

MANAGE TAX DOLLARS MORE EFFECTIVELY

DEMONSTRATE RESPECT FOR OPINIONS OF OTHERS

KEEP PEOPLE INFORMED

CLEARLY ESTABLISH THE NEED
FOR A NEW BUILDING

When he finished, the group decided that, even though more Customer Values would certainly emerge if the discussion continued, they would stick with this list for the sake of keeping the exercise reasonably short.

"Next, what we would need to do is get some feedback on these Values," said One Voice, "to find out how

The Customer would rate each one. We would conduct a telephone survey in the community, with questions something like these." He read through them:

• On a scale of 7 to 1, where 7 is "vitally important" and 1 is "not at all important," how important is it to you that the leadership exhibit the following qualities?

• On a scale of 7 to 1, where 7 is "excellent" and 1 is "poor," how well does the present leadership perform on these qualities?

"Okay," said One Voice. "I suggest we reconvene on Monday night to finish this session, and to develop our hypothetical plan for gaining The Customers' trust and support, which the leadership will need before it can build this school."

* * *

On Monday, One Voice had transcribed the list of Customer Values onto a house-shaped chart similar to the one that The Architect had used to explain the design and planning process.

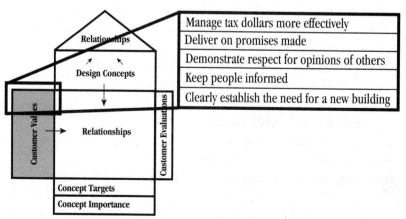

"Well folks, here we have the side wall of our 'building of trust,'" said One Voice, "And with it we are going to begin to construct the rest of the building. As you can see, along the left side of the house, we have listed the five hypothetical Customer Values that we agreed on at our last meeting. As you've probably noticed, they are in a different order than they were on our pad last week. That's because The Architect and I assigned ratings to them of relative importance and performance, just as there would be numerical values assigned to them if we'd actually conducted the phone survey.

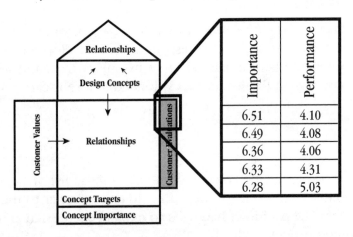

"For instance, the Customer Value listed as 'Manage tax dollars more effectively' received the highest rating of impor-tance from our hypothetical phone survey and, at the same time, scored relatively low in performance. On the other hand, the Customer Value listed as 'Clearly establish the need for a new building' was rated as relatively high in importance and also relatively high in performance. In any event, it's not so important that you understand how we arrive at those statistical calculations as it is that you see that we have here objective structure and some prioritization as we proceed."

"What's next?" asked The Voice of the Superintendent.

"This is going to be a good demonstration of how the process will work," said The Architect. He and One Voice had met over the weekend and now he fully understood how the Customer Values they had developed would be used to design a program for building trust. "Today, we're going to pretend we are the Trustbuilders' Planning Group. We have here some wonderful Voice of the Customer information which with to work. Let's take each of these Customer Values and try to conceive of Solutions, what we refer to as Design Concepts in the case of an actual school building, to meet each of these Customer expectations. For instance, what must or could we do to offer convincing proof that we are managing tax dollars more effectively?"

"In business you perform a regular audit," said The Voice of the Business Leader.

"Could you expand on that thought?" asked The Architect.

"Well, I know that we have periodic public audits of our district's records, but why not get some local business people involved in doing an entirely third-party audit of our district using methods and practices respected by those of us in the private sector?" proposed The Voice of The Business Leader.

"Great idea," said The Architect. "Let's add it to the top room of our house. Now, what we're doing is constructing the Solutions layer of our trust-building."

The group worked through the Customer Values, asking of each, "What must we do to offer convincing evidence that we are delivering on this value?"

Several suggestions pertained to school district finances. The Voice of the Taxpayer championed the idea of presenting financial reports in ways that the public could better understand. The Voice of the Teacher suggested they host a series of district-wide seminars on "School Finance 101."

It didn't take long for the group to open up and become very creative. The Voice of the Business Leader suggested that they could gain more trust if the district showed more leadership by using information technology in student instruction.   The Voice of the Parent suggested that often everyday problems cost the district credibility. "When parents walk in these buildings and see how over-crowded and chaotic they are during school hours, it doesn't garner much confidence and respect for the leaders' management abilities," said The Voice of the Parent. The Voice of the Superintendent confessed that they could improve their credibility by improving their approach to long-range planning.

After several hours of discussion, One Voice returned to the house-shaped graphic and recorded the following Solutions along the top of the diagram.

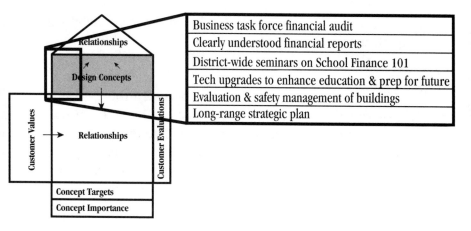

| | Business task force financial audit |
| Clearly understood financial reports |
| District-wide seminars on School Finance 101 |
| Tech upgrades to enhance education & prep for future |
| Evaluation & safety management of buildings |
| Long-range strategic plan |

"Now comes the fun part," said The Architect. "Let me introduce you to some new symbols. First, we have The Bullet.

"As we work through this diagram, we'll use The Bullet to represent a strong relationship between the Customer Value and the Solution, which is numerically expressed as a 9.

"Then there's The Circle. The Circle will be used to symbolize a medium relationship, or a 3, between the Customer Value and the Solution. Next there's the Triangle.

"We'll use The Triangle to symbolize a weak relation-ship, or a 1, between the Customer Value and the Solution."

"What if there's no relationship between the Customer Value and the Solution?" asked The Voice of the School Board President. "For instance, The Business Leader's suggestion that we upgrade our information technology capabilities doesn't have any relationship to The Taxpayer's idea that we need to demonstrate respect for the opinions of others."

"If that's truly the case, we'll use the good, old-fashioned Goose Egg," said The Architect.

"I'm still unclear on how this works," said The Voice of the Student.

"Let's take the first brick on the wall," said The Architect. "Look along the left side of the house and you'll see the first Customer Value is 'Manage tax dollars more effectively.' Do you see that?"

The Student nodded.

"Look along the top of the house. Do you see where we listed the Solution 'Business task force financial audit'?"

Everyone was following closely.

"Let me ask you, "Does that Solution' have a strong, medium, weak or no relationship to the Customer Value 'Manage tax dollars more effectively'?" The Architect questioned.

"Strong."

"Strong."

"Strong."

"Definitely strong."

"Bullet," said The Voice of the Coach. The group erupted in laughter.

"Right! A Bullet, which means a 9. You're quick learners," said One Voice.

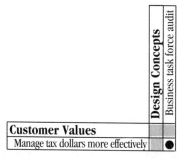

In all, there were 180 intersections between Customer Values and Solutions. Not all of the relationships were as easily reconciled as the first one. When the group came to the relationship between the Customer Value 'Demonstrate respect for opinions of others and the Solution 'Technology upgrades,' The Voice of the Teacher suggested it was a weak relationship.

"I disagree," said The Voice of the Business Leader. "I think progress in this area suggests great sensitivity to the opinions of people like me. I would say it is a strong relationship. I would give it a 9."

"Bullet," said The Voice of the Taxpayer.

"Goose Egg," said The Voice of the Student.

"Okay, everyone, which is it?" asked One Voice.

"I'll upgrade you to a 3 on this one if you'll promise me an upgrade later," said The Voice of the Student.

"Hey! That's not the way this is supposed to work," said The Voice of the Superintendent. "You're the referee, call a foul!"

Everyone chuckled. They were having fun.

"Seems to me the object of the game is consensus," said The Voice of the Coach. "Does it matter how we get there?"

"It's true that all we need to do is to agree on which number it is," said One Voice. "But it's not really a barter system. What is important is to have some good give-and-take before we agree on the final number."

"So how do we feel about this relationship between 'respect for opinions' and 'technology assets'?" asked The Architect.

"I could live with a Circle," said The Voice of the Business Leader. "It's at least a medium relationship."

"The Business Leader helped me understand a relationship I couldn't see," said The Voice of the Teacher. "I agree it's a medium relationship. Give it a Circle."

"I don't know," kidded The Voice of the Coach. "I'd be interested in seeing what concession I could gain on the next box if I held out for a Goose Egg on this one."

The Parent took The Coach by the hand and jokingly gave his arm a twist. "Uncle! Uncle!" cried The Voice of the Coach. "You can have your Circle. Just let me go!" The Architect marked the house accordingly and they moved on through the rest of the relationships.

* * *

Design Concepts

Financial
- Business task force financial audit
- Clearly understood financial reports
- District-wide seminars on School Finance 101

Facilities/Technology
- Tech upgrades to enhance education & prepare for future
- Evaluation & safety management of buildings

Planning
- Long-range strategic plan

Customer Values		Importance	Performance
Manage tax dollars more effectively		6.51	4.10
Deliver on promises made		6.49	4.08
Demonstrate respect for opinions of others		6.36	4.06
Keep people informed		6.33	4.31
Clearly establish the need for a new building		6.28	5.03

Concept Targets

- One time per year
- Available at Central Office
- Four times per school year
- Graduation/employment progress
- Ongoing
- Activities with time frame

Concept Importance

| 10.933 | 10.447 | 9.941 | 8.774 | 8.093 | 13.783 |

One Voice rose to interpret the completed house
that was constructed from the group's hypothetical
exercise. "Let's look at what this objective map tells
us about building trust between the leaders of this
school district and its Customers. Focus if you will
on the Solutions that have the greatest number of
Bullets. These are the bricks in the house that give
the greatest support to our objective of building
trust. These Solutions stand out as the most important. If the leadership does nothing else, they should
do these things, and if the district doesn't have the
resources to do them all, we should at least provide
for doing the most important ones."

One Voice used a color marker to highlight the
leading Solutions.

"Of course, at this point the leadership would have
to walk their talk. It's one thing to conceive these
things; it's another to live them," said One Voice. "If,
however, this leadership group honestly and actively
got behind these programs, then I think they could feel
secure in knowing that they'd done the best they
could in gaining the trust we need to take this building
project forward."

"I'd say our leaders have their work cut out for them,"
said The Voice of the Business Leader.

"I'm exhausted," said The Voice of the Coach. "Let's
go home."

"I think we've done our fair share this evening," said
One Voice. "But as we're leaving, let me tell you that
what you experienced in tonight's session is just a

sampling of what it will require to build The Schoolhouse of Quality. Remember what I told you:

You will be tired, but you will end up invigorated.

Chapter 5

THE VOICE AT THE TOP

Several weeks had passed. The process of planning the new school building design had begun. Focus groups with various customer segments were being held throughout the district. Research surveys were taking place. At a meeting with One Voice and The Architect, The Voice of The Superintendent spoke positively of the progress that was being made.

"We're getting such wonderful response from the trust-building programs we've initiated," said The Voice of the Superintendent. "The esprit de corps throughout the district is better than it's been since I've been here. I have to tell you that I'm feeling like one of the most confident school superintendents in the state."

"That's a good thing, because we're going to need every bit of confidence and enthusiasm that you've got to get this school building off the ground," said The Architect.

"What do you mean?" asked The Voice of the Superintendent. "I thought this was a big collaborative enterprise. Why does it all of a sudden fall back on me?"

"It doesn't fall back on you," said The Architect. "It begins with you. A company cannot buy its way to quality–it must be led there by top management."

"You're the top management here," said One Voice. "Everyone else is either here because they work in the district or because they have strong personal interest in the quality of education. As you know, ultimately you'll be the one held accountable. That's why there can be no stronger advocate for this program and what it stands for than you."

"I've never coordinated a process like this before," said The Voice of the Superintendent. "In the past, I've just sat down with my people, gained some of their feedback, then met with the architects to get some drawings done. What do I have to do differently this time?"

"I've given this a great deal of thought," said One Voice. "I'd suggest that you do it exactly as the CEO of my company did it when our Quality program was initiated."

"How did the CEO do it?" asked The Voice of the Superintendent.

"There are many, many details to be concerned about, but it seemed to me that our CEO did four things very well. Here, I made a list."

The Superintendent took the sheet from One Voice's hand and studied it. Here's what was on it.

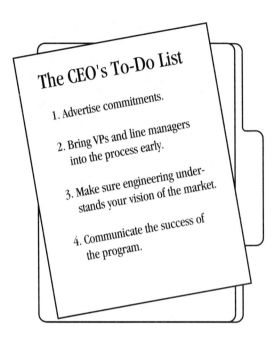

The CEO's To-Do List

1. Advertise commitments.

2. Bring VPs and line managers into the process early.

3. Make sure engineering understands your vision of the market.

4. Communicate the success of the program.

"I can see how this was a workable agenda for your CEO, but I don't see how it works for me," said The Voice of the Superintendent. "We don't advertise. I don't have any vice presidents or line managers. There isn't an engineering staff. This is fine for a private-sector approach, but we have a different set of circumstances here."

"Not really," said One Voice. Using a pencil, One Voice marked several revisions to the handout.

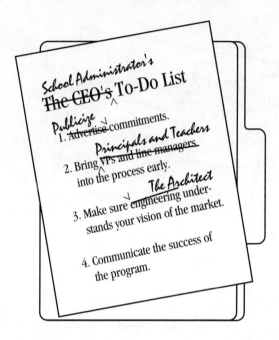

School Administrator's
~~The CEO's~~ To-Do List

Publicize
1. ~~Advertise~~ commitments.

Principals and Teachers
2. Bring ~~VPs and line managers~~ into the process early.

The Architect
3. Make sure ~~engineering~~ understands your vision of the market.

4. Communicate the success of the program.

"Yes, I see," said The Voice of the Superintendent. "Tell me more about how your CEO launched a House of Quality approach at your company."

"From the day the CEO gathered employees to discuss Quality, it was clear that the company was heading in a new direction. It was obvious to everyone that the commitment to Quality was not just something that was going to be expected of us, but something in which the CEO believed very deeply and regarded very personally."

"So should I call everyone together and explain this entire process?" asked The Voice of the Superintendent.

"If you do it the way our company did it, you won't work through every detail of the process at the very beginning. I think it would be best to roll out the process in general terms. This is going to be a very open, interactive process, but providing too many details at the outset may inhibit progress. For instance, we got bogged down very early trying to understand every step of the research phase. It cost us several weeks. In retrospect, we would have done better to just get started," said One Voice.

"One thing that I think would work well for your school," One Voice continued, "would be doing some very broad-based communicating right away. Let's get a news release out to the local reporters who cover the school district, and I'm sure you have some kind of a newsletter or other means of getting information to teachers and home to parents, don't you?"

"Of course we do," said The Voice of the Superintendent. "We can get something out yet this week."

"Before you do that," said One Voice. "I suggest you proceed on The School Superintendent's 'To-Do' number 2. You need to get the principals and faculty together. These meetings will be crucial for building the all-important base of support among this key customer group and for generating excitement for this process. If our CEO hadn't had the vice presidents and line managers on board early, we would never have made any progress in getting the kind of company-wide buy-in that was required to make things happen."

"How do you suggest we handle these meetings?" asked The Voice of the Superintendent.

"I'd keep them short," said The Architect. "You'll need to be prepared to answer the basic questions that are sure to be raised about this process."

"For example?"

"'What is 'The Schoolhouse of Quality'?"

"And how would you answer that?"

"I would tell them that our aim is to design a new school building that fulfills and hopefully exceeds the expectations of The Customers," said The Architect. "Make sure they understand that The Customer is defined as anyone with a stake in the facility, so it not only includes teachers, students and parents, but School Board members, business leaders and the community at large. The Schoolhouse of Quality process will provide clear direction to our architects and, therefore, let us design a facility that meets everyone's needs and expectations."

"What other questions should I be prepared to answer? Won't I be expected to explain how the process works?" asked The Voice of the Superintendent.

"You will, but that's the area in which you want to be careful about getting too bogged down in process details," said One Voice. "Explain that the process begins with one-on-one interviews and Customer focus groups to establish Customer Values. Remember, these '10,000 feet' values are linked to concepts. You know, we're flying way up here for starters." One Voice's hand glided through the air like a jet.

"You do have to explain the basic ideas of Customer Values and Design Concepts," said The Architect. "You will also have to sketch out the role that the Community Design Team plays in this process."

"The Community Design Team seems to me to be a very touchy subject," said The Voice of the Super-intendent. "Who chooses those who get to be on the Community Design Team?"

"You do with our help," said The Architect. "Your most important role throughout the entire Schoolhouse of Quality process will be working with us to identify the types of people who will sit on the Community Design Team. You will then actually recruit 15 to 20 of these individuals. These people will meet for two all-day sessions to brainstorm Design Concepts and then evaluate them in light of the Customer Values."

"The Bullet and Circle thing?"

"Precisely," replied The Architect. "There will be two factors to consider as we work together in forming this team. First, we want to select representatives from all your constituencies. In addition to School Board members, teachers, students and their parents, don't forget to include business leaders and people who live in the community and who either don't have children or send them to other schools. Second, this is an intense, team-oriented, idea-generating exercise. You want energetic, cooperative, creative people."

"Make sure you don't select people with axes to grind," said One Voice. "We had a couple of line managers who got passed over for promotions six years ago, and they tried to get their justice at the expense of our Quality process. You have to be very careful about this kind of thing."

"I would think it would be important to select people who can be good ambassadors for our project, wouldn't you?" asked The Voice of the Superintendent.

"That is very important," replied One Voice. "The success of the program nourishes itself as the participants share their positive experiences with others through word of mouth."

"Let's step back a second," said The Voice of the Superintendent. "Your 'To Do' number 3 suggests that I need to spend some serious time briefing you. At this point, what more could I possibly tell you about our situation?"

"It's true that we've been with this building project for a while now," answered The Architect. "You've already supplied the basic information about facilities, staff size, enrollments, your board members, the community leaders and the demographic information. I guess we could skip that part."

"I wouldn't," said One Voice.

"Really? But what else do we need to cover?" asked The Architect.

"The human side," said One Voice. "I suggest you two go off somewhere and talk about the subjective things.

The Superintendent ought to take you back into the recent history of the district and the community. Find out where some of the bodies are buried, as they say. What are the good things that are happening? What agendas are hidden, and who's hiding them? How's the football team doing this season?"

"Quality in a company or in a school district emerges from the contributions of many people doing many different jobs well," One Voice continued. "The more holistic a view that both of you possess about this project, the better equipped both of you will be to sweat its details."

"I don't know about you," said The Architect, "but I could be a lot more holistic over a burger and fries."

"Why don't you and I go find some, and then start talking about the human side of this project?" asked The Superintendent. "One Voice, would you care to join us?"

"No," One Voice answered. "Your partnership is critical to the success of this approach. I'd prefer to let it develop on its own."

"Have it your way," said The Voice of the Superintendent. "I will say that at the beginning of our meeting today I was quite unclear as to my role in this whole thing, but you've both contributed to my having a greater degree of clarity, and I thank you."

"No need to thank me," said One Voice. "You'll recall one of the truths of this process."

You will be confused, but you will experience clarity.

Chapter 6

THE SEARCH FOR THE CUSTOMER'S VOICE

"Thanks a lot, Chuck," said The Voice of the Coach into the telephone receiver. "This will just about do it. I'm heading for that meeting with all the ammunition I'll need." The Coach hung up the phone.

"Who was that?" asked The Voice of the Assistant Coach.

"That was Coach Chuck over at Nextville High. Look at this. I've been working on this nonstop for three days." The Coach opened a three-ring binder filled with diagrams, lists and financial spreadsheets.

"What is it?" asked The Voice of the Assistant Coach.

"I've talked to every coach and athletic director at every school within 50 miles of here," said The Voice of the Coach. "I know what facilities they have, how much they cost, what's working and what's not working – the whole enchilada."

"What are you going to do with all this?" asked the puzzled Voice of the Assistant Coach.

"I'm going into battle," said The Voice of the Coach. "Tomorrow's the day of the school staff's focus group, and when I get to the table, there isn't going to be anyone better prepared to defend their interests than me. Yes, I think we're going to do just fine."

* * *

The conversation among the Moms and Dads lined up alongside the soccer field during practice was usually small talk: laments over busy schedules, expensive gym shoes and too many school fund-raisers. Today, it was different. Everyone along the sideline was focused on what The Voice of the Parent was telling them.

"...And then we'll build a consensus around those Design Concepts that best meet the Customer Values," said The Voice of the Parent who had been invited to participate in a focus group and who had read some background material on the process.

"Well, I hope they improve the traffic and parking situation," said The Voice of a Mom. "I feel like I take my life into my hands every time I drive onto the property."

"And if I were building a school," said The Voice of a Dad, "I would design it to be more of community center, particularly in the evenings. Do you know how many programs in this community are in desperate need of a place to meet? We just don't have any place like that in our community, and it seems like we should get double duty out of our new..."

"Look out!" cried The Voice of a Soccer Player.

The Voice of a Dad was stopped mid-sentence when a soccer ball bounced off the side of his head.

"Are you all right?" asked The Voice of the Parent.

"Yeah, I'm all right," said The Voice of the Dad. "I don't know whether that was meant to add emphasis to a good idea or to suggest that it was a stupid idea," he said as the others laughed with him.

"Oh, I've come to believe there really aren't any bad ideas," said The Voice of the Parent. "It's just an example of one of your needs and desires as a Customer of this new building. Hey, while we're waiting on the kids, why don't we write down some of these thoughts? Then I'll be prepared when I go into the Parents' focus group that I've been invited to participate in."

The Moms and Dads were only too willing to cooperate, and as the soccer practice continued, they conducted an ad hoc research session at the sidelines.

* * *

Every day at high noon, The Voice of the Business Leader could be heard announcing the unofficial commencement of the lunch hour at The Club.

"This is going to be my lucky day!" said The Voice of the Business Leader.

"Oh, every day is your lucky day," shot back The Voice of the Retired Industrialist. Such bickering was a ritual that the two had perpetuated for years for the entertainment of the other guests in the dining room.

"No, I'm serious today," said The Voice of the Business Leader as he took a leather and brass seat at the table. "Today, I am involved in a great and noble cause: the education of our young people, our hope for tomorrow."

"What are you talking about?" asked The Voice of the Young Entrepreneur.

"I've been invited to participate in the businesspersons' focus group for our new school design project," said The Voice of the Business Leader. "And I tell you, at last I feel that I'm going to have an opportunity to chart a proper course for our schools."

"Well, I hope you're able to do something about the basics," said The Voice of the Corporate Manager. "We spend way too much money every year, when all we need to do is teach people to read, write, add and subtract."

"The 'Three R's,' that's what we called 'em," said The Voice of The Retired Industrialist. "You go in there and get that school back on course, old friend."

"That was already on my list," said The Voice of the Business Leader.

"I don't know," said The Voice of the Retailer. "Basic skills are essential, but I think we need to focus on character, things like respect, responsibility and virtue."

"I'm ahead of you there, too," said The Voice of the Business Leader. "In fact, I wrote a short essay entitled 'A New Paradigm for Education: The Voice of a Business Leader.' My trade association journal has just featured the article on its cover. I had it reprinted and have made enough copies for every member of the focus group. I've also put together a short slide program, which I plan to share at the meeting."

"Well, I'm encouraged," said The Voice of the Chamber of Commerce executive. "How about if we continue this stimulating conversation over lunch?" The exchange between all the various businesspeople gathered for lunch that day at The Club focused on their needs and desires for the new school.

* * *

One Voice and The Architect arrived early in the morning to begin setting up for the local businesspeople's focus group. When they entered the darkened room, they heard The Voice of the Business Leader.

"...And finally, respect, responsibility and virtue. These are the things that matter most. Oh! You startled me!" said The Voice of the Business Leader as the lights in the room came on.

"We're sorry," said The Architect. "We didn't expect anyone to be here so early."

"I came down a little early to run through my slides and my presentation for today," said The Voice of the Business Leader.

"Your slides?" said One Voice.

"Your presentation?" said The Architect.

"Yes, I thought I could best share my point of view if I took the opportunity to organize my thoughts into a short presentation," said The Voice of the Business Leader.

The Architect glanced at One Voice. One Voice smiled and shrugged his shoulders.

"I'm glad you've taken this responsibility so seriously," said The Architect. "I'll tell you what, would you mind helping us set up for the meeting, and when the appropriate time comes, we'll see where your presentation may fit into the session?" The Business Leader happily accommodated.

Within the hour, a cross-section of the business community was assembled. The Architect began the meeting.

"Today we are going to concentrate on establishing the Customer Values that..."

"Values! I was hoping we would get to that first," said The Voice of the Business Leader. "We won't succeed at all in our endeavors unless we can first instill a sense of values in our young people. Respect and responsibility, that's where it's at. We must build character. Would this be an appropriate time for me to share my slide program?" asked The Voice of the Business Leader.

"Not just yet," said The Architect. "What I would like to do first is clarify, again, what we mean by a Customer

Value, particularly as it relates to our assignment. One Voice, maybe you could help here."

"Here's a little cheat sheet of definitions I prepared that you'll want to keep close at hand during this process," said One Voice, distributing flyers to the group. "Look at the first definition."

> *Customer Value: In the context of a particular relationship (e.g., Student-to-Teacher), a customer value states what would need to be reflected in the building design to ensure that an outstanding educational process could occur.*

"Issues like character and responsibility are critically important," said One Voice, "but we also have to focus on issues that address how the building can enable the education process. It's not simple to design respect and responsibility into a building, but we can develop concepts that encourage and foster responsibility and respect. We just need to start at a more practical level."

The Business Leader seemed somewhat deflated as it appeared that the opportunity to deliver the slide presentation was evaporating, but at the same time seemed to acknowledge the practicality of One Voice's direction.

* * *

At the school staff focus group the following day, One Voice had just finished delivering a similar speech. The Voice of the Coach spoke up.

"Okay," said The Voice of the Coach. "I know what

you're talking about. You want specifics, details and practical stuff. Now, over at Nextville they have a 400-seat gymnasium, but if they move in their portable bleachers they can push that to 600. We have two choices in terms of the portables. The Acme brand cost a little bit more, but..."

The Architect raised a hand. "Hold on a minute, Coach. We also don't want to run all the way to nuts-and-bolts specifics. A good way to begin to get a grasp on what a Customer Value is, is for us to look at all the various relationships in the educational process and why they're important. For example, let's start with 'Student-to-Teacher.' What are some of the others?"

The school staff focus group completed its inventory of relationships, and The Architect listed their findings on a flip chart:

STUDENT-TO-TEACHER
STUDENT-TO-STUDENT
STUDENT-TO-PRINCIPAL
STUDENT-TO-BUSINESS COMMUNITY
STUDENT-TO-PARENT
STUDENT-TO-SELF
TEACHER-TO-PRINCIPAL
TEACHER-TO-PARENT
PRINCIPAL-TO-PARENT
TEACHER-TO-TEACHER
TEACHER-TO-SELF
PRINCIPAL-TO-OTHERS
PARENTS-TO-COMMUNITY
PARENT-TO-SELF

* * *

A similar list was made at the next focus group, which involved parents from the school district. The Architect was leading that group through the same definition of Customer Values.

"Now, as we think of these relationships," said The Architect, "what would need to be reflected in the building design to ensure that an outstanding educational process could occur within one or more of these relationships?"

The Voice of the Parent spoke. "Well, yesterday I was at soccer practice, and one of the issues that came up was that the driveway and drop-off area at the existing school isn't safe."

"Where would you place that issue on our relationship list?" asked The Architect.

"I guess it would be Student-to-Parent or Parent-to-Self. It speaks to the Parent's fundamental concern for safety," said The Voice of the Parent.

"Okay, let's list that under Student-to-Parent, for now," said The Architect. "One Voice, how would we express that as a Customer Value?"

"You might say something like, 'Parents easily and safely drop off children at the school,'" One Voice explained.

"This is a very good example!" said the Architect. "It is an issue of importance to Customers that relates to how the building can enable the process of education within the Student-to-Parent relationship."

* * *

As each focus group worked its way through each meeting, a challenging but friendly tug-of-war took place between the lofty and the specific. Just about the time the school staff focus group would define a series of excellent Customer Values, The Voice of the Coach would begin reciting from the product specifications in the three-ring binder. Eventually, The Voice of the Teacher said, "Oh, would you just put that binder away? Don't you understand that stuff is way too specific for what we're trying to do today?"

"But I worked hard on collecting this information," said The Voice of the Coach. "Do you mean to tell me it's all meaningless and all my effort is worthless?"

"I believe The Coach has a point there," said The Voice of the Principal. "He's engaged in considerable reflection over this initiative, and it seems that at some point he should share his conclusions."

"Relax," said One Voice. "Don't you see that the process is working? You all have been very actively engaged in this. Each of you has been reaching into your own communities and interest groups in your different ways. Through you, the various customers' voices are being heard. Let's look at the long list of Customer Values we've developed during our session and then you tell me whether you think you've been heard."

After about two hours of discussion, the walls of each focus group room ended up lined with flip chart pages. Each page was titled with a different Customer relationship. The Architect reviewed the Customer Values that had been listed on the first page. "Look at what we've done here with the Student-to-Teacher relationship," said The Architect.

"The exciting thing," said One Voice, "is that if you go through this list, what you'll recall is that almost every single person in this room made a contribution."

The Architect moved around the room and recited the Student-to-Teacher Customer Values on each list:

• *Access to appropriate equipment, including technology, to make learning more fun and interactive*

• *Students concentrate and hear teachers without distraction of outside noise*

• *Students engage in one-to-one instruction with teachers in classroom*

• *Students and teachers enjoy a physically comfortable classroom environment*

• *Students have the opportunity to work in groups with teacher support*

• *Teachers can arrange classrooms for a variety of approaches to instruction*

• *Students and teachers have appropriate classroom storage for supplies and projects*

• *Students and teachers are exposed to the outside for upbeat classroom feeling*

One Voice complimented each focus group. "I know it's been a long session, but we have accomplished a great deal. What you see on these walls is the raw material of our design process. As a next step, these Customer Values will be quantified through our survey research. Then, after the Community Design Team gets together, you'll see how we'll use these Customer Values to develop Design Concepts for delivering on the Values."

Chapter 7

BRICK BY BRICK

In order to keep the school staff members removed from the interruptions of their daily business, the site of the Community Design Team meeting was held in the civic room at a local bank. The 15 people around the large table at the center of the room included The Principal, The Teacher, The Parent, The Student, The Taxpayer, The Business Leader, The Coach and The School Board President. At the main table were copies of the School-house of Quality diagrams listing the Customer Values identified by the focus groups and survey research. The same diagram was also displayed on several laptop computers and an oversized version sat on an easel at the front of the room.

"This is the day we will test the very limits of your patience and endurance," said One Voice.

"Oh, that sounds frightening," said The Voice of the Parent. "What are we going to do?"

One Voice gestured toward The Architect. "My friend, I will leave it to you to outline today's agenda."

The Architect placed a huge board on the easel. It was the Schoolhouse diagram, but it was substantially more complex than any they had seen previously. "Remember this?"

"Yes," said The Voice of the Business Leader. "But it sure was a lot smaller the last time we saw it. When you showed us the Schoolhouse the last time, I think we only had about six panels in the side wall. How many are there now?"

"The are 38 Customer Values listed along the left side of the Schoolhouse, and they've been organized by the various relationships we discussed."

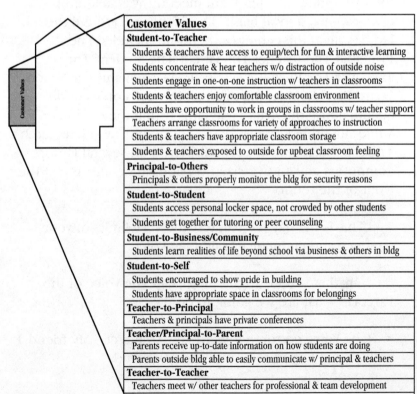

Customer Values

Student-to-Teacher
Students & teachers have access to equip/tech for fun & interactive learning
Students concentrate & hear teachers w/o distraction of outside noise
Students engage in one-on-one instruction w/ teachers in classrooms
Students & teachers enjoy comfortable classroom environment
Students have opportunity to work in groups in classrooms w/ teacher support
Teachers arrange classrooms for variety of approaches to instruction
Students & teachers have appropriate classroom storage
Students & teachers exposed to outside for upbeat classroom feeling

Principal-to-Others
Principals & others properly monitor the bldg for security reasons

Student-to-Student
Students access personal locker space, not crowded by other students
Students get together for tutoring or peer counseling

Student-to-Business/Community
Students learn realities of life beyond school via business & others in bldg

Student-to-Self
Students encouraged to show pride in building
Students have appropriate space in classrooms for belongings

Teacher-to-Principal
Teachers & principals have private conferences

Teacher/Principal-to-Parent
Parents receive up-to-date information on how students are doing
Parents outside bldg able to easily communicate w/ principal & teachers

Teacher-to-Teacher
Teachers meet w/ other teachers for professional & team development

"What you see listed along that side of the Schoolhouse is The Voice of the Customer," said One Voice. "It's what I've been talking about since we first began this journey. Now, we need to get down to delivering on those Customer Values."

"That's why we call you a Community Design Team, because, today, you're going to do some designing," said The Architect.

"I thought that was your job," said The Voice of the Taxpayer. "We're not designers. What are we paying you for if we're going to design this thing?"

"Make no mistake," said The Voice of the Architect. "My colleagues and I at Tymeliss, Frugill, Eeger & Arteest will certainly earn our keep as we relate our professional expertise and training to the feedback you will share today. You'll see."

"Well, don't look to me for any design input," said The Voice of the School Board President. "Everyone has always told me that my tastes are very eclectic. I'm not sure I would want to impose my odd sense of taste on the entire district."

"I'm color blind," said The Voice of the Coach. "I don't see how I can be much of a designer. Do you want me to come back when we start talking about the athletic facilities?"

The Architect raised a hand to try to bring the murmuring crowd to some level of calm. "Hold on, everyone, it's not what you're thinking. What we're going to rely on you to do is to isolate some Design Concepts. Remember when we talked about them?"

"Just what do you mean by 'Design Concepts'?" asked The Voice of the Teacher.

"Let's put a definition on the board just as we did with the definition of a Customer Value," replied The Voice of the Architect, turning to the board with marker in hand.

> *Design Concept: An idea measurable in time, distance or space that can tangibly deliver on a Customer Value or series of Customer Values. While it is measurable, it is not necessarily the measurement.*

"So, my 600-seat gymnasium is a Design Concept?" asked The Voice of the Coach.

"Not exactly," answered The Voice of the Architect. "Certainly a particular seating arrangement is a Design Concept, and your idea of portable seating is an even better example. Six hundred seats, on the other hand, is the measurement. Why don't we refer to that as the Target Concept to shoot for?"

"What we're trying to do here," said One Voice, "is identify design concepts without being so specific that we don't leave any room for our architects to lend their creativity and experience to our needs. Maybe it will be helpful if we can just dive right into the Schoolhouse."

"I think you're right," said The Voice of the Architect. "Let's all look at the Schoolhouse diagram." In addition to the large poster of the Schoolhouse diagram resting on the easel at the front of the room, The Architect had given every member of the Community Design Team a miniature version to use as a reference. "If you look at the left side of the house, the first set of Customer Values contains those listed under the relationship of Student-to-Teacher. Is everyone following me? What was the most important Customer Value under that relationship?"

"Well, if I'm reading this correctly," said The Voice of the Business Leader, "it would be that notion about having the right equipment and technology to make learning–How did the Customers say it?–more fun and interactive?"

"That's right," said The Voice of the Architect. "Inside the Student-to-Teacher relationship, a Customer Value that was identified was:

• *Students and teachers have access to the appropriate equipment, including technology, to make learning more fun and interactive.*

"Now, let's try to come up with some Design Concepts that can deliver on the Customer Value of students and teachers having access to equipment, including technology, to make learning more fun and interactive."

"Just put a computer on every desk," said The Voice of the Student.

"Now, see, I think that is a good example of where this whole approach is going to break down. There is just no possible way that we can afford to put computers on every desk," said The Voice of the School Board President.

"There isn't any reason for the approach to break down over the suggestion to put a computer on every desk," said The Voice of the Architect. "The Student's voice needs to be heard as part of our process, but so does yours. The Student understands that obviously the best way to give teachers and students access to technology is to put a computer on every desk. Your voice, as President of the School Board, however, also needs to be heard, because you have a more informed sense of the resources we'll have available to deliver on Customer Values. Where, then, does that lead us?"

"We still need to deliver on the Customer Value," said The Voice of the Parent.

"Precisely," said One Voice. "And what does that mean?"

"Seems like we'll need to get creative here and find some middle ground," said The Voice of the Teacher.

"Okay," said The Voice of the Principal. "What if rather than having a computer on each desk, you at least provided a data connection to each room? You would be able to plug computers into a network throughout the building so that you could use a smaller number of computers in a larger number of spaces, and add more later as you need them."

"Now there's an excellent example of a Design Concept," said The Voice of the Architect. The concept was written along the top of the Schoolhouse diagram.

"But making learning fun and interactive isn't just about technology," said The Voice of the Parent. "I think we put too much hope in technology today. I agree that learning needs to be more fun and interactive, but aren't there ways we can deliver on that Customer Value without relying on machines? I don't know, it all seems kind of cold and impersonal to me."

"I agree," said The Voice of the Teacher. "The thing that I think gets in the way of creating fun and interactive approaches to learning is the classroom and its teaching equipment. For the most part, it doesn't matter if I teach in the room at this end of the hallway or at that end. In many cases, they're all the same. You almost need to be able to go into a classroom and organize it the way you want it for your lesson, and then move on to the next classroom and be able to do the same thing."

"Well then," said The Architect, "isn't that a Design Concept?"

"What do you mean?" asked The Voice of the Teacher.

"I mean, shouldn't we write something up here that goes something like this?"

• *Movable, multipurpose work and storage spaces.*

"Oh, it would be great if we could do that," said The Voice of the Teacher. "I could get into this."

"I told you that would happen," said One Voice. "Remember what I said:

You will be tired, but you will be invigorated.

"I'm glad you're feeling invigorated," said The Voice of
the Architect. "We have plenty more Customer Values to
work through. You'll need that energy and enthusiasm.
Now that we finished the Student-to-Teacher relationship,
let's look at the Principal-to-Others relationship where
you will find a Customer Value that is expressed as:

• *Principals and others properly monitor the building
for security reasons.*

"So, what Design Concepts can we come up with to
deliver on this Customer Value?"

"We need some way to monitor the entrances, outside
hallways and public areas of the building. That's where
we run into trouble today," said The Voice of the Principal.

"Okay," said The Architect. "That's a Design Concept.
Anyone else have an idea?"

"I can tell you we need to control access to the gymnasium and the rest of the building," said The Voice of
The Coach. "I don't know how many times we've had
to interrupt basketball practice to deal with someone
who's wandered into the gym looking for the auditorium after hours."

"That works both ways, Coach," said The Voice of
the Teacher. "When we're practicing in the auditorium
for the fall theater arts performance, we often have
people from the visiting team looking for your junior
varsity games."

"Well, then I'd say we have more in common than we probably thought," said The Voice of the Coach.

One Voice jumped up excitedly. "There it is again! Remember when I said:

You will be stubborn, but you will develop new respect for the opinions of others.

"Who you callin' stubborn?" asked The Voice of the Coach.

"Maybe you should change that to 'overly turf protective,'" joked The Voice of the Teacher.

"Hey! I'm on your side on this one," said The Voice of the Coach. They slapped palms together in a high five as the rest of the team roared with laughter.

"How do we take what The Coach and The Teacher have just addressed and express it as a Design Concept?" asked The Architect.

"I never know what door to come in," said The Voice of the Parent. "Maybe if we had some kind of clearly distinguished visitor's entrance?"

"What about a visitor's center?" suggested The Voice of the Taxpayer. "You know, kind of like when you cross over the state line when you're on a trip on the interstate. Maybe we could be that obvious about it. It might avoid a lot of confusion. That is, of course, if we can afford to pay for it." The Design Concept of a separate visitor entry with a welcome center was added to the list at the top of the Schoolhouse diagram.

For the next several hours, the Community Design Team worked through every one of the 38 different Customer Values. Led by the insight and experience of The Architect, the conversation was rich with both innovation and the revelation that, like The Coach and The Teacher, many people in the district shared needs, problems and desires that they had never realized.

For instance, The Principal, The Student and The Teacher engaged in some creative give-and-take that resulted in a Design Concept calling for a centrally located student center and conferencing area. This related to The Student's value of needing a place in which to show pride; The Teacher's need to have a place to meet with other teachers, parents and administrators; and The Principal's need for improved building security.

As they considered the Customer Values of "Students getting together for tutoring and peer counseling" and "Students being able to learn the realities of life beyond school," The Parent and The Business Leader took the lead in suggesting that space be dedicated to personal and career counseling, and that programs be taught and facilitated by people outside the regular school staff.

In all, by focusing on each Customer Value one at a time, and asking themselves "How do we want to deliver on it?" The Community Design Team came up with 36 different Design Concepts.

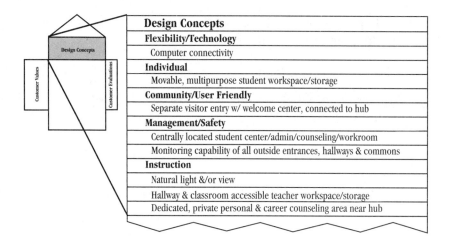

Design Concepts
Flexibility/Technology
Computer connectivity
Individual
Movable, multipurpose student workspace/storage
Community/User Friendly
Separate visitor entry w/ welcome center, connected to hub
Management/Safety
Centrally located student center/admin/counseling/workroom
Monitoring capability of all outside entrances, hallways & commons
Instruction
Natural light &/or view
Hallway & classroom accessible teacher workspace/storage
Dedicated, private personal & career counseling area near hub

The Architect could see that the team was exhausted. "That will do it for today, folks. Tomorrow we'll come back and complete our house by going back through every brick in the house where each of the 38 Customer Values intersects with each of the 36 Design Concepts.

"Oh, that's the thing we do with the doodads and thingamabobs," said The Voice of the Coach.

"That's right," said The Architect. "Bullets, Circles, Triangles and Goose Eggs."

"Before we adjourn," said The Voice of the Taxpayer, "I'd just like to say that despite some of the differences of opinion that have been expressed throughout this process, I think we should be pretty proud of ourselves. I think we're starting to come together around some very good and powerful ideas."

"I agree," said The Voice of the Coach. "We're performing like a great team. It's exciting."

The other members of the Community Design Team expressed similar sentiments of enthusiasm and encouragement to each other.

One Voice smiled. "Remember what I told you:

Your opinions will be challenged, but good ideas will prevail.

Chapter 8

BULLETS AND GOOSE EGGS

As the Community Design Team gathered for its second day of collaboration, a new sense of esprit de corps was evident among them. The Taxpayer and The Principal had discovered a shared enthusiasm for the Design Concept of a welcome center, and were overheard discussing just how that idea might be worked into the school building.

The Parent and The Teacher were genuinely excited about many of the Design Concepts that, if implemented, would make them even closer co-workers in the job of educating the children.

The Business Leader had already begun to think about how the material on responsibility, respect and virtue might be reorganized and presented differently to students in one of the new conference areas set aside for student exposure to outside resources.

As The Architect, One Voice, The School Board President and The Principal walked into the room, The Architect whispered to the other three, "Let's not get over-confident, but I think we're beginning to see a school building come together." The Principal gave a smile and a thumbs-up to the School Board President.

The Architect called the meeting to order. "Ladies and gentlemen, today we're going to wear you out."

"I thought we did that yesterday," said The Voice of the Teacher.

"Yesterday was nothing compared to what we have to work through today," said One Voice. "Remember, we have identified 38 Customer Values and now we have 36 different Design Concepts. That means we have 1,368 interrelationships or 'bricks' in the Schoolhouse."

"And?" asked The Voice of the Taxpayer.

"And we're going to look at every single one of those interrelationships," replied One Voice.

"But that will take us forever!" exclaimed The Voice of the Student.

"It won't take us forever, but it will take us several hours. So let's get started," said The Voice of the Architect.

"As we look at each of the 36 Design Concepts listed across the top of the Schoolhouse, we will travel down the diagram and rate each and every Customer Value," explained The Voice of the Architect. "As we do so, we will ask this question: To what extent does this Design Concept deliver on this Customer Value?

"If the Design Concept has a strong relationship to delivering on the Customer Value, then we will mark that intersection with a Bullet.

"The Bullet, by the way, carries a numerical value of 9. If the Design Concept has a medium relationship to delivering on the Customer Value, we will mark that intersection with a Circle, which has a numerical value of 3.

"If the Design Concept has a weak relationship to delivering on the Customer Value, we will mark the intersection with a Triangle.

"The Triangle carries a numerical value of 1. Finally, if the Design Concept has no relationship to delivering on the Customer Value, we will either mark it with a Goose Egg, or just leave the space blank.

"The Goose Egg, of course, carries no numerical value. Are we ready, and does everyone understand?" asked the Architect.

"I'm not sure I fully understand, but I never understand the rules to a board or card game when they're read to me," said The Voice of the Parent. "If we'll just jump in and start playing, it should come to me pretty quickly."

"Then let's jump in," said The Architect. "Let's take the first Design Concept, which we define as 'A centrally located student center and conferencing area.' Does everyone remember that concept from yesterday?"

All nodded in agreement.

"Now, moving down the left side of the Schoolhouse, let's go to the Customer Value defined as 'Students and teachers will have access to appropriate equipment, including technology, to make learning more fun and interactive.' Is everyone focused on the intersection between the Design Concept and the Customer Value?" asked The Architect. "Okay. So now let me ask the group, 'To what extent does a centrally located student center and conferencing area deliver on students and teachers having access to equipment, including technology, to make learning more fun and interactive?'"

Design Concepts
Centrally located student ctr & conf area

Customer Values
Students & teachers have access to equip/tech for fun & interactive learning

"I'd say it has no relationship," said The Voice of the Business Leader.

"I guess it all depends on what goes on in the student center and conferencing area," said The Voice of the Teacher. "I mean, the activity inside the center could end up being fun and interactive, and you could utilize technology in that area."

"You're right," said The Voice of the Business Leader. "I hadn't thought of it that way. But it certainly isn't a strong relationship."

"I didn't say it was strong," said The Voice of the Teacher. "I just said it was related."

"So what is it, team?" asked The Architect.

"Medium," they answered in unison.

"Medium it is," said The Architect.

"Uh, that would be a Circle, wouldn't it?" asked The Voice of the Student.

"Circle or the numerical value 3, whichever is most comfortable for you," said The Architect. "Let's look at the next Customer Value. To what extent does a centrally located student center and conferencing area deliver on 'Students being able to concentrate and hear teachers without distraction of outside noise?'"

"Zip."

"Zero."

"Goose Egg."

"If everyone is in agreement, we'll move on to the next," said the Architect. "We only have 1,366 to go."

"Oh, great," said The Voice of the Coach.

The team found that the Design Concept of a centrally located student center and conferencing area bore no relationship to the next dozen Customer Values listed on the Schoolhouse diagram. They concluded, after some discussion, that the concept related strongly to the Customer Value expressed as "Students encouraged to show pride in building." When they finally worked their way down to the areas of the Schoolhouse diagram that dealt with Teacher, Principal and Parent relationships, they found that the Design Concept related very strongly to several of The Customer Values, including:

✔ Principal and others monitor the building for security
✔ Teachers and Principal have private conferences
✔ Teachers meet with Teachers for team development

As the group worked through each Design Concept, there were long strings of intersections in which the Design Concept seemed to bear absolutely no relation-ship to the Customer Value, and then several intersec-tions would suddenly light up with Bullets indicating strong relationships. Such was the case when they attempted to relate to the Design Concept of "Movable, multipurpose student workspace/storage" to the Customer Values:

- *- Students engage in one-on-one instruction*
- *- Students have opportunity to work in groups*
- *- Teachers arrange rooms for variety of approaches*
- *- Students have space in classroom for belongings*

About halfway through the day, The Voice of the
Parent interrupted to say, "The thing I'm finding very
interesting is the way in which, as we move through
these bricks, we're starting to see the way some Design
Concepts deliver on a lot of Customer Values, even
though the Design Concepts may not have been original-
ly conceived to deliver on anything but one of them."

"Yes," said The Voice of the School Board President,
"I've noticed that, too. Look at how many Customer
Values the Design Concept of "Hallways and classrooms
accessible to teacher workspace" relates to. That single
Design Concept delivers, albeit moderately, on 13 of the
38 Customer Values."

"The point you make is at the very essence of this
process," said One Voice. "Take the example you just cited.
What this exercise is going to do is take each of our Design
Concepts and represent them very visually in terms of their
overall importance to delivering a Schoolhouse of Quality.
When we hand this finished diagram over to The Architect
and his colleagues, one of the things we will be saying to
them is this, 'Make sure hallways and classrooms are accessible
to the teachers' workspaces,' because that one idea is
packed with customer-perceived Quality."

"I wonder if I could take this approach in serving my customers?" asked The Business Leader excitedly. "I bet if I did,
my company would end up with more of them satisfied."

"Makes sense," said One Voice. "That's the way world-class companies design Quality into their products and services."

"And we're also designing Quality into our school building," said The Voice of the Parent. "I'm sure I won't be the only Parent who sees the value of this approach."

"You know, I'm even beginning to get a whole lot more comfortable with paying for this building," said The Voice of the Taxpayer.

"Talk about a coup," whispered The Principal to The School Board President. They chuckled.

"I hate to rain on everyone's enthusiasm," said The Architect. "I'm excited about the new building, too. In fact, I am very eager to get to my office to start working on the plans. Unfortunately, before we can, there are 639 more intersections to complete."

A collective groan was heard through the room as The Architect began again, "To what extent does the Design Concept expressed as 'Natural light or view' deliver on the Customer Value of..."

Customer Values	Centrally located student center/admin/counseling/workroom	Monitoring capability of all outside entrances, hallways & commons	Computer connectivity	Movable, multipurpose student workspace/storage	Separate visitor entry w/ welcome center connected to hub	Natural light &/or view	Hallway & classroom accessible teacher workspace/storage	Dedicated, private personal & career counseling area near hub	Importance	Performance
Student-to-Teacher										
Students & teachers have access to equip/tech for fun & interactive learning	○		●	●			△	○	6.46	3.41
Students concentrate & hear teachers w/o distraction of outside noise				△					6.41	4.10
Students engage in one-on-one instruction w/ teachers in classrooms			●	●					6.07	3.78
Students & teachers enjoy comfortable classroom environment			△	○		●			6.05	3.68
Students have opportunity to work in groups in classrooms w/ teacher support			●	●					5.90	4.20
Teachers arrange classrooms for variety of approaches to instruction			○	●			△		5.88	3.82
Students & teachers have appropriate classroom storage for belongings			△	○			●		5.82	3.25
Students & teachers exposed to outside for upbeat classroom feeling						●			5.41	3.63
Principal-to-Others										
Principals & others properly monitor the bldg for security reasons	●	●	△		●		○	○	6.28	3.66
Student-to-Student										
Students access personal space not crowded by other students				○			△		5.78	2.56
Students get together for tutoring or peer counseling			●	○				●	5.41	3.88
Student-to-Business/Community										
Students learn realities of life beyond school via business & others in bldg			○	△	△			●	5.87	3.71
Student-to-Self										
Students encouraged to show pride in building	●		△	△	●	△			6.05	4.02
Students have appropriate space in classrooms for belongings				●					5.97	3.75
Teacher-to-Principal										
Teachers & principals have private conferences	●		△					○	5.34	4.29
Teacher/Principal-to-Parent										
Parents receive up-to-date information on how children are doing	△		△		△		○	○	6.07	4.45
Parents outside bldg able to easily communicate w/ principal & teachers			△					○	5.76	4.38
Teacher-to-Teacher										
Teachers meet w/ other teachers for professional & team development	●		○				△		5.82	3.78
Concept Targets	One area	All areas	Every curriculum	One per student	One area at main entrance	All habitable areas	One per two clsrms	One area		
Concept Importance	15.159	1.662	17.634	33.316	7.077	11.886	10.725	8.891		

Design Concepts: Management/Safety · Flexibility/Technology · Individual · Community/User Friendly · Instruction

Chapter 9

WHAT'S AN ARCHITECT TO DO?

"Well, well, well," said Frugill, "the Gallup of architecture has returned. Have you finished your polling? Tell me, oh wise seer, what do the latest ratings tell us about how we ought to do our job?"

The Architect was perturbed, but before he could react to Frugill's harassment, Eeger jumped in. "Get off his back. Look, there are a lot more Design Team meetings now being held with various school departments, and I've been sitting in on some of them. The initial Schoolhouse diagram is helping to guide these discussions. We're now coming into this project with more conceptual raw material than we have had on any project we've ever done. In any event, we're very much committed to this process at this point, so the best thing for us all to do is to review the results of The Schoolhouse of Quality exercise and see where they lead us in finally getting this building out of the ground."

Frugill smirked and shrugged.

For the next two hours, The Architect briefed, or debriefed as it were, the firm on The Schoolhouse of Quality process. Every Customer Value was described. Every Design Concept was reviewed. Finally, The Architect explained the statistical model used to display the prioritization of the values and Design Concepts. On the wall in front of all the TFE&A associates was the completed Schoolhouse of Quality diagram with all its Bullets, Circles, Triangles and Goose Eggs and the related Design Concepts of the yet-to-be-designed school building.

"I've never seen such a mess in all my career," said Frugill. "This has all been a sweet experience for all of us," he said sarcastically, "and I'm glad that every man, woman and child in the district has had their say, but can we please begin drawings on this project?"

Tymeliss stood and, scowling at Frugill, said, "That will be enough! I admit I've had my reservations about this whole procedure from the beginning, but after having seen this presentation, I can tell you, Frugill, that now you're just being stubborn and prima donnaish. Just look at what's up on that board. It's an architect's dream. Solving the conceptual puzzle that's mapped out before us is the very essence of our profession. My mind has just been whirling as The Architect has been describing this feedback."

"I'd be interested in knowing what's been whirling through your mind," said The Architect.

"Well, we're charged with attacking the physics of all this. We now have to take all of these needs and desires and try to satisfy them within certain limits of time, space and money. That's supposed to be our area of expertise. And if you think you're so good at that," Tymeliss said, looking directly at Frugill, "let me suggest to you that what you have before you is going to challenge you to the limits of your abilities."

"That's what I've been saying," replied Frugill testily. "It's a hodge-podge. How can we possibly bring order out of all that chaos?"

One Voice appeared in the doorway to the conference room. "It's not a hodge-podge, and it's not chaos. These Customers of yours have already brought order out of their conflicting needs and desires. If you'll just study the diagram, you'll see that. We're essentially at a place where you as architects are either going to use your professional skills and talents to design the building these Customers want with their help, or you're going to design the building you want irrespective of their expressed needs and desires. May I remind you that you have already taken the latter course and failed."

"I agree with Tymeliss," said Eeger. "Once the departmental groups have finished meeting, we'll have everything we need. We'll just have to figure out how to extract a design from what's on the map."

"I guess I still don't see why you are so enthusiastic," said Frugill.

"Let me give you something to think about," said Tymeliss. "Look at the Schoolhouse we have here. They want to improve the public access to the building with one centralized entrance. At the same time, they want to zone certain areas for after-hours access, and then you have this thing going on where they don't want people who are coming to an athletic event to get mixed up with those who are coming to a theater arts rehearsal."

"That's right, and they want this centralized student and career center. How do we accomplish all those things?" asked Arteest.

"Remember your training and your education," said Tymeliss. "Aren't these the very kinds of challenges you had to wrestle with in order to gain your degree? I think this represents a very stimulating challenge for us. Look, I've already started to conceptualize some of the blocks." Tymeliss held up a small piece of gridded paper on which was drawn four blocks labeled "center," "gym," "theater," and "access." "Now, how are we going to get these things tied together in a way that satisfies these people?"

Frugill nodded. "Hmm, I see what you mean. You know, the other thing that I don't really know is how we're going to provide services like plumbing, electrical and HVAC to all of these flexible spaces they want. I guess I have to admit that I am kind of intrigued by the challenge of figuring out how to make this happen."

"You wouldn't believe the kind of new thinking we had to do at our company when we saw the first Quality reports," said One Voice. "Our first impressions were that these things just couldn't be done. They didn't represent the way we'd always designed and manufactured products. But the process forced us to think differently. Our CEO gave us no choice. The Team was committed to delivering on the Customer Values. And when we were done, we had new products that no one else in the market offers. It's been very much part of our success."

Frugill and Tymeliss huddled over the small piece of gridded paper. They spoke so softly to each other that no one else could hear them.

"Do you mind sharing with us what you two are stirring up over there?" asked The Architect.

"Well, Frugill may have something here," said Tymeliss. "Why don't you share your idea?"

"There's no way they're going to get this single entrance they want," said Frugill.

"Oh, you're just being negative again. If you simply don't want to participate..." The Architect was interrupted by Tymeliss mid-sentence.

"Hear this out," said Tymeliss. "Frugill is not being uncooperative. There's a legitimate point to be made here."

"Anyway," continued Frugill, with a dramatic sigh at the interruption. "What if we could accommodate three Customer Values at once? What if we designed a facility with three entrances?"

"Three entrances!" exclaimed The Architect. "They'd never buy that."

"Not so fast," replied Frugill. "You create a centralized entrance that leads into that welcome center they want.

Then you create two other entrances at separate ends of the building: one that leads to the gymnasium and the other that leads to the auditorium."

"Yes!" said Eeger. "And the welcome center could be adjacent to the student and career center. This component could be two stories, giving them the kind of centralized hub they're looking for."

"Having sat through these sessions, I can tell you that our friend The Coach is going to be happy with that solution," said One Voice.

"The Coach?!" exclaimed The Architect. "What about The Teacher? If we move that music and theater program to the opposite end of the hall, The Teacher is going to be ecstatic."

"Ladies and gentlemen, once we have the departmental input, we'll have a royal opportunity to prove that we really do know how to design," said Tymeliss. "There must be over a hundred such puzzles in that diagram. As Eeger said a while ago, there's a school building in there, and we're the only ones involved in this process who know how to get it out of that chart and onto the construction site."

"I guess instead of telling us how to do our jobs," confessed Frugill, "this process will prepare us to do our jobs."

"I like the way you used your creativity to deliver on more than one Customer Value at the same time," replied Arteest.

"Again, I know I've been the naysayer," said Frugill, "but to be honest, I don't think I could have conceived the multiple entrances idea without seeing those Values and Design Concepts colliding with each other on the chart. After Tymeliss started talking about this being a classical architectural dilemma, it sparked something in me. I apologize for being so difficult. I truly believe we now have the chance to be more creative."

"I think the way this process sets up to be able to deliver on more than one value at a time is part of its beauty," said The Architect.

"You're absolutely right," said Tymeliss. "It's not that we've generated a list of innovative parts that we'll subsequently toss into a kit that we'll call a building. What this process has yielded is a perspective on all the things they want, in order of the priority in which they want them. But, it also clearly shows the relationship of those needs, desires and priorities to each other. By our being able to see that perspective, we're better able to conceive and propose. Again, in all my years in the profession, I don't think I've ever felt better prepared to do a job."

"So what you're saying is that it's not that we'll necessarily deliver the longest list of cool Solutions, but rather that we'll deliver a package of features that delivers on the longest list of Customer Values," said Arteest.

"Precisely," said One Voice. "And if you do that, I promise you that you'll have one very happy set of customers on your hands. Your firm's architectural expertise is unmatched, and I've already seen many instances where your team of pros has extracted insights from this process that would have been lost on me and everyone else. In your hands, this process will certainly result in a wonderful facility."

"Then are we ready to hear what the departmental groups have to say?" asked Frugill.

"You tell me," replied Tymeliss with a smile. "Are you ready to use their input to start some drawings?"

Replied Frugill, "I have never been more ready, nor better prepared."

Chapter 10

MONEY TALKS, TOO

Several weeks later, TFE&A and the Community Design
Team were finally able to join forces to present a comprehensive new school building design to the School Board.
Had The Architect left that first meeting and returned to
the drawing board immediately, the firm would have been
back to the School Board over a month ago. As it was,
The Schoolhouse of Quality had required an investment
of time, but The Architect was content knowing that it
had been time well spent. He had never been more eager
to present a new plan to a client.

As the members of the School Board, citizens, teachers,
parents and other school officials were taking their seats,
The Architect recalled his last, torturous presentation to
this group. "Finally," The Architect thought to himself, "I'm
here with a plan the whole community had a say in."

The Architect wasn't the only one proud of the plan
to be presented. Tymeliss, Frugill, Eeger and Arteest were
all seated on the platform with The Architect, as were The
Superintendent and the entire Community Design Team
including The Principal, The Teacher, The Parent, The

Business Leader, The Taxpayer, The Coach and The Student.

Members of teams from departments such as Science, Drama and Humanities were present, too. Each planned to cover some aspect of the presentation, because each had contributed meaningfully to the final design.

The School Board President gaveled the meeting to order. "Ladies and gentlemen, you all know why we're here. The Community Design Team is here to present the final results of our Schoolhouse of Quality process and the design of our new school building."

The Architect began by explaining the origin of the Customer Values, then turned the microphone over to The Student. "One of my first ideas," said the nervous, yet proud Voice of the Student, "was that a great way to make learning interactive and fun was to just put a computer on every desk. However, this didn't exactly fly with the whole team." The audience laughed appreciatively.

The Architect then explained the information technology infrastructure planned for the new building. "Although, with existing resources, we're not able to put an individual computer on each desk, you can see how we have established the network and connections throughout the building to allow a generous amount of new hardware to be moved to different classrooms and labs throughout the building."

The Voice of the Business Leader spoke. "This Design Concept is very similar to the approach we have in one of our warehouse operations. We don't have computers throughout the building, but we move them where we need them and are equipped to plug in wherever we are at any time."

"The Business Leader shared that with us during the Community Design Team meeting," said One Voice. "And that contribution helped to inspire this Concept."

The Architect and the Design Team continued to lead the Board and the audience through the design. As they did, The Architect stopped to correlate each design idea back to The Schoolhouse of Quality diagram displayed next to computerized 3-D models of the new building.

Next, The Voice of the Teacher spoke. "Right now, I share a classroom space with three other teachers. We needed a way for each of us to do our own thing in that same space. The solution was to have the ability to rearrange the room quickly after each class period."

Arteest then explained how the firm had managed to bring utilities to the flexible classroom spaces designed to serve the widest variety of curricula and teaching styles. "I have to tell you, ladies and gentlemen, with all these movable fixtures we've designed in, I have never had a more difficult time figuring out how to get water and electricity to a classroom. But, we did it!"

The Voice of the Parent took over. "Confusion with building access was a big issue among a lot of Moms and Dads and with a lot of Teachers. So I think all of you will agree with me that the rather unconventional approach we took to building access is a great solution."

Then it was Frugill's turn. "The facility is designed with three separate entrances," he began. "Maybe that sounds odd at first. But if you bear with me for a moment and watch the Schoolhouse chart as we unveil this design, I think you'll be surprised at just how hard we've worked to satisfy The Voice of the Customer."

The Architect leaned over to One Voice and whispered, "Did you ever think you'd hear Frugill talking like that?"

"Frugill believes," One Voice replied.

When Frugill had finished with the explanation of the multiple entrances Concept of the design, The Voice of the Parent added, "I hope this satisfies everyone as much as it satisfies me. I particularly like what we've done with the automobile traffic. I think visiting this building will now be a lot safer."

"This plan also satisfies me," said The Voice of the Principal. "The centralized hub created near the welcome center is going to work better for both building administration and for relations with the general public."

Said The Voice of the Teacher, "I'm also happy you've taken our loud-mouthed Coach and the sweaty athletes and you've put them way at the opposite end of the building."

"Let me just say that this loud-mouth is glad to be at that opposite end," replied The Voice of the Coach. "I think it's clear that, for the first time, we're truly presenting a school plan that will satisfy The Customer."

"Well, I'm not satisfied," said a voice from the front of the audience. It was The Voice of the Missing School Board Member. This Board Member had elected not to participate in The Schoolhouse of Quality process and, though all Board Members had been kept informed at each step along the way, tonight was really the first time The Missing School Board Member had truly focused on the process. "Has anyone seen the price tag on this project? I'm sure there will be no way we can afford it.

"Now, I don't want to rain on anyone's parade," continued The Missing Board Member as he rose from his seat. "I know there have been a lot of people who have given a lot of time and energy to getting us to this point and, it's true, I wasn't one of them. I'm not suggesting we throw out the entire plan, but I'm sure we can't afford this building as it's designed."

A nervous murmur moved through the audience.

The Missing School Board Member pointed at the floor plan. "For instance, you see those little areas between these classrooms?"

"Yes," said The Architect, "those are adjoining spaces between classrooms for teacher workspace, small student work teams and Teacher-Parent conferences, but..."

The Missing School Board Member harrumphed. "Unnecessary! These are just a luxury. If you take those out and use that space more efficiently, you'll save a lot of money. I've been involved in some construction before. Am I right?" He took his seat.

"With all due respect, I disagree," said The Architect, finally able to be heard. "One of the major goals of The Schoolhouse of Quality process is to work within the resources available. The plan you see here isn't a result of jacking up the building price. It's a result of good planning and creative thinking being used to reconcile conflicting opinions and needs.

Looking directly at The Missing School Board Member, The Architect continued, "There's a good reason for everything on this plan, and especially for those small spaces between classrooms. Look at where those spaces are on this Schoolhouse diagram. Of all the Design Concepts on this diagram, this one scored very high in terms of its ability to deliver on the Customer Values driving this project. Get rid of those spaces, and you are choosing not to listen to The Voice of the Customer. Luckily..."

The Architect walked to an easel and unveiled the final budget for the new building.

"...The Schoolhouse of Quality lets you listen to The Voice of the Customer, and the voice of your wallet!"

The Community Design Team, the School Board and the audience laughed and applauded. The Missing School Board Member sank a little lower in his chair.

"So here's how we were able to stay within budget," said The Architect. "Use the Schoolhouse diagram. Just as it tells us that those spaces between classrooms are powerful in delivering on the Customer Values of this project, it tells us those Design Concepts which, relatively speaking, deliver less strongly. So we could go back to the drawing board and deal with these financial issues creatively with these priorities in mind, rather than surgically removing a concept so vital to customer satisfaction."

All of the members of The Community Design Team nodded approvingly to each other. The Coach patted The Architect on the back.

"And let's not forget," said The Voice of the Taxpayer. "I'm as tightfisted as the next person, but I've always tried to buy Quality. In this case, you really do get what you pay for. In fact, you get a lot more. I think we've got a design this community can wrap its arms around. I mean, look at us. We've never been able to agree on anything, and a few minutes ago The Architect had us all standing and applauding. We've got something here."

As if on cue, the audience began to applaud again.

At that moment, The School Board knew that the district was going to get its new building. The Architects knew that they were going to get to construct the building they had designed. And One Voice, and the many people who had given their time and energy to the process, knew they were going to build a better school.

Chapter 11

ONE VOICE AMONG MANY

It had now been almost two years since the School Board had unanimously approved the design for the new school building. Hundreds of people were now gathered on the lawn in front of the new building, which was constructed just as it had been designed. A gala dedication ceremony was under way. The marching band had performed a repertoire of pop and patriotic tunes, The Mayor and other local dignitaries had taken their bows and basked in the community's enthusiasm for the new school. The keynote speaker for the dedication was at the podium.

"Whether you are in goods or services, today we have all come to understand the ultimate source of differentiation in the marketplace is Customer-defined Quality." The speaker was One Voice's boss, The CEO. "At our company, we learned this lesson the hard way. But today we understand, better than ever, that the attributes of Quality reside in the minds of our customers. We dedicate this marvelous new school building today knowing that the school district has embraced the same principles we use in the private sector to serve our customers, to serve the needs and desires of this community."

Seated on the platform behind the speaker were the School Board President and Members, The Superintendent and the entire Community Design Team. The only one not present was The Student, who had graduated shortly after the completion of the design, and was now enrolled, not surprisingly to many on the Team, in the school of architecture at the state university.

Also on the platform was The Architect representing the firm of TFEA&L. That's right. With the stupendous success of this project, The Architect was promoted to partner and his name, Lissen, was added to the firm's shingle. As Lissen enjoyed this pinnacle moment in his career thus far, he was reminded of his own early skepticism of The Schoolhouse of Quality process. As The CEO spoke, Lissen's mind wandered to the words once spoken by One Voice:

You will be skeptical, but you will be convinced.

One Voice had been invited to sit on the platform, but elected instead to sit with family members and enjoy the dedication from the perspective of the audience.

The CEO continued, "... and now we must understand how important it is that we teach these same fundamentals to the students who will occupy this great structure: that excellence is a noble and worthy aspiration, and that other people matter. We are moving into a new economy of services, information and intangibles, in which not only the Quality of our manufactured goods matter more than ever, but, more importantly, the Quality of our service, the depth of our caring and the sincerity of our interest in and involvement with those around us. A commitment to Customer-defined Quality built this school. Now let's make Customer-defined Quality part of its curriculum."

After The CEO's remarks, the crowd was divided into three groups to tour the new school building. The Coach led the tour at the gymnasium end of the building. The Business Leader led one at the welcome center entrance. And The Teacher led a group to the entrance near the auditorium. One Voice joined Lissen and The CEO to wander freely among the three tours. First, they toured the student and career center. There they met The Business Leader.

"These are the real things one requires to succeed in business today," said The Voice of the Business Leader. He was presenting his slide show on respect and responsibility to a group of students and their parents in the small conference room designed for student interaction with the school's business partners. The Business Leader interrupted the presentation when One Voice and the others walked into the room. "Excuse me, ladies and gentlemen, but here is Mr. Lissen, our architect; my dear friend, One Voice; and of course, you all know The CEO.

"Please continue with your presentation," said Lissen. "I know you've been working on it for some time," he said with a wink and a smile.

The Business Leader blushed. "I am glad to have the attention of these very well informed students and parents.

Do you know that my colleagues at The Club have agreed to take turns offering mini-seminars on all aspects of business and professional life? We couldn't even begin to do it without this wonderful facility. I must say that this project was a somewhat laborious task and I was at times quite impatient, but I feel some accomplishment and take genuine satisfaction in knowing that I had something to do with all this. Thank you very much for involving me."

As One Voice, Lissen and The CEO walked toward the auditorium, they were met by The Superintendent and The Principal. "Mr. Lissen, I must tell you that the administrative hub back behind you is just one the nicest Design Solutions of any building I've ever been in. It is going to make my life and job so much easier," The Voice of the Principal said.

"That's a good thing, since you're going to be with us for a while," said The CEO. The day before the dedication, the School Board had announced that The Principal had been given a new multi-year contract.

The Superintendent laughed. "It's a funny business, this field of education. Twenty months ago I was close to being ridden out of town on a rail, and today...well, let's just say One Voice has made me a big believer in this Schoolhouse of Quality thing. When we began, frankly I was a little nervous about all these people challenging my preconceived ideas for this building. But in the end, good ideas prevailed, as they should. Now, we're developing Schoolhouse diagrams on the curriculum, the food service operation and the transportation program. Before we're done, there'll be a half dozen other areas we'll use this process on."

"Before you're done?" asked The CEO with puzzlement. "One Voice, haven't you told them?"

"I guess I haven't been as emphatic as you are back at the plant, but what The CEO is trying to say is, you're never done. Quality is a matter of continuous improvement. Once you've succeeded at satisfying and exceeding Customer expectations, new needs and desires begin to take shape. Now that you've made a commitment to satisfying The Customers, you need to keep them that way."

At this point, The Teacher walked up, preparing to turn one of the tours over to another guide. "Good afternoon, how are you? It's so good to see you," said One Voice.

"I'm great, but I'm exhausted," said The Voice of the Teacher. "You wouldn't believe what we've been through getting ready for today. Well, I guess in the larger sense, you know as well as anyone else. After all, you did tell us that we would be exhausted, but in the end we would be invigorated. And I am! On the last tour, a group of our guests were from a very respected regional community theater, and they were so impressed with our theater they want to make a substantial contribution to our drama program in exchange for being able to use the facility. Imagine that! They're asking me to use my theater. Or I guess I should say 'our' theater, but honestly I think of it as mine because there are so many of my ideas in there. I'm so thrilled."

As they turned to walk back to the gymnasium end of the building, The CEO said, "One Voice, it seems we have some very satisfied customers here." One Voice just beamed.

By the time they got to the gymnasium, the tours were beginning to disband and all of the members of the Community Design Team were gathered around a buffet table of refreshments set up outside the athletic department office. The Coach came out of the office and raised his hands in a victory sign when he saw The Teacher, The Student, The Principal, The Superintendent, The School Board President, The School Board Member, The Taxpayer, The Business Leader, The Parent, The CEO, Tymeliss, Frugill, Eeger, Arteest, Lissen and One Voice.

"Hey!" cheered The Voice of the Coach. "It's my team!" He put one hand on top the other and invited the guests into a huddle, where they shouted, "1-2-3 Team!" All roared with laughter.

"Do you know, I just had the head football coach and athletic director in here from Nextville High, and they were just green with envy. We've done things to that gymnasium that no other school has done. We're all just blown away by how Lissen and his colleagues dealt so creatively with all the key Customer values."

"The Coach sure has come a long way, hasn't he?" said The Voice of the Teacher.

"Okay, okay," said The Voice of the Coach. "I confess I was as stubborn as an old mule, but by the time we were done, One Voice was right: I learned a great deal of respect for the opinions of others. I'm happy with what I've got going on in that gym, but I'm just as happy with what we've got going on all around this building. The manner in which TFEA&L executed the design with The Customers' input was simply amazing."

As the group cheerfully reviewed both the success of the project and the success of the day, One Voice quietly made his way toward the exit. The CEO walked quickly to catch up.

"I know you're uncomfortable with taking credit, but you must know that you've made a tremendous difference here," said The CEO.

"Thanks. It's been a great experience, but the real credit goes to the many design teams and, of course, Lissen and his colleagues. I think it's been fascinating how we could take the Quality concepts you've taught us back at the plant, and make them work here at the school," said One Voice.

"You know why they work, don't you?" asked The CEO.

"In some respect, I guess it's just common sense," said One Voice.

"No doubt about that," said The CEO. "But, the only way these concepts work is when people like you begin to think of themselves not just as employees and volunteers, but as owners. You took such passionate ownership of these concepts back at the plant, you weren't afraid to advocate them here before the School Board. And because of it, this community has an outstanding new facility. I guess it is true what they say, 'One voice can really make a difference.' You have."

One Voice looked back at the still-chatting Voices of the Customers. "We all have."

They walked in silence for a moment. Then The CEO put a hand on One Voice's shoulder. "You know, I've been thinking about making some changes in plant management..."

Afterword

Intuitively, we all know that the physical structures we call schoolhouses can have a tremendous impact on the quality of teaching and learning that goes on inside them. That's why there are such passionate and diverse opinions when a school district faces new construction or renovation projects.

While building or renovating schools should and can be a source of community participation and pride, these projects are too often a source of division and disappointment. Meaning well, some districts invite opinions and suggestions, and get plenty of them. But with no way to prioritize needs or reach consensus, the end result is a long list of irreconcilable wishes. In other situations, district leadership takes a "we know best" approach only to discover — after the project is completed — that the community felt otherwise.

We developed The Schoolhouse of Quality process as a means of establishing consensus around schoolhouse needs, priorities and budgets. That way, when the doors of a new or renovated school are opened, the community can embrace the end result because they helped design it. The Schoolhouse of Quality is a proprietary process that goes beyond brainstorming sessions or town hall meetings. Its sophisticated and proven methods, outlined in the story of One Voice, capture and define the community's "values" as they pertain to educational facilities and related concerns.

The roots of The Schoolhouse of Quality can be found in the 1970s and '80s when American businesses received a wake-up call from the Japanese. During this time, Japanese companies, particularly car and electronics manufacturers, clobbered their American competitors and dominated markets worldwide. In short, the Japanese were delivering a higher quality, more reliable product and — this was the real clincher — at a more reasonable price. Japan's secret weapon: Total Quality Management, or TQM.

TQM is based on a simple premise: True quality is defined by the customer. If the customer's needs and expectations are met or surpassed, then quality is achieved. Anything short of that is unacceptable.

American companies, and many others throughout the world, were quick to catch on to and implement TQM programs of their own. As a result, these companies became more competitive, won back customers and began to give the quality-minded Japanese a run for their money.

While proven and accepted in the private sector, TQM is relatively new to the public sector. Only recently have public entities like school districts begun to think about the people they serve as customers. When they do, it changes the way they think about and approach virtually everything they do.

When you think about it, schools have many customers. Perhaps students and their parents come to mind first. However, teachers, administrators, the business community and adults who live in the district but who don't have children in district schools are all customers, too.

Listening and responding to the voice of the customer doesn't mean catering to every whim. A company can't, for instance, cut its prices in half simply because a customer requests it; a school district can't build an Olympic-sized pool simply because the swim team requests it.

However, when many voices begin to blend into one, it's a very different story. When many customers begin to complain that products are unreliable, smart companies take immediate steps to improve product reliability. When school districts hear from many different customer groups that an integrated new media center would be a valued facility improvement, smart districts will make it happen.

Our firm has been using The Schoolhouse of Quality process since 1990. It was born of our own self-funded pilot program for which we conducted comprehensive research. Along the way, we have helped numerous school districts build community consensus around single and multiple facilities. When our design work is complete, we — with the help of some of the district's customers — present our work to the community. You'll often hear architects talk of "defending" their work in such situations. With the voice of the customer driving our designs, neither we nor the school boards that hire us need to take a defensive posture.

When the community tours a school we helped them design, we hear the same phrases repeated over and over: "This is just what I envisioned." (Read: "It meets our expectations.") "I can't believe we got all of this within our budget." (Read: "You prioritized our needs properly.")

We accomplish our work at a cost that is considerably less than the national average spent on facility design and construction. Better need not be more expensive. Take clearly established, agreed-upon needs and priorities and then add a healthy dose of design experience and creativity. You end up with a Quality facility — within budget.

The Schoolhouse of Quality is not limited to schoolhouses. The process is also used for technology, curriculum and district-wide planning, to name a few. For instance, one application of the process called Trustbuilders helps districts identify how they can foster trust and confidence in the community. Once achieved, such faith in the leadership inspires progress and facilitates consensus building. This trust is especially important for those districts that must go directly to voters for funding.

Our customer-focused approach is not about abdicating budgeting, curriculum and other decisions to the community. The process only works when the experts — administrators, teachers, architects, etc. — are empowered and entrusted to use their training and expertise, but always with the customer in mind. As architects, interior designers and planners, we find that customer input doesn't stifle our creativity, but rather it stimulates and focuses our imaginations.

Despite all the gloom-and-doom talk, American education is strong. But it can and must get better. This will only happen when school districts routinely seek out and listen to that one important voice. The voice of the customer.

We hope you enjoyed the story of One Voice, and we invite you to write us with your comments, suggestions and questions.

> *Gerald S. Hammond, FAIA*
> President
> *Stephen H. Schwandner II*
> Schoolhouse of Quality Partner
> Steed Hammond Paul Inc.

Author contact information:

Steed Hammond Paul Inc.
1014 Vine Street, Suite 2100
Cincinnati, Ohio 45202
voice: 513.381.2112
fax: 513.381.5121
e-mail: ghammond@shpinc.com
World Wide Web: http://www.shpinc.com

Acknowledgments

The Schoolhouse of Quality would not have been created nor blossomed into a nationally recognized and respected process without the contributions of many colleagues. They include, but are by no means limited to: Lauren Della Bella who was instrumental in getting our firm and its customers to understand and embrace this new and better way to design schools; Michael Dingeldein, AIA, whose architectural talents and willingness to abandon trusted, but worn-out paradigms is inspiring; and Dale Heidotting, AIA, whose creative genius first proved this process could be applied to school architecture.

The Schoolhouse of Quality circa 1990 is not the process as we know it today. Many people along the way have provided insights and ideas that have enabled us to improve the process. The ultimate beneficiaries of these improvements have been our country's children. We thank each of these collaborators, their names too many to list here.

In addition to all that we have learned from and shared with superintendents, school board members, parents, principals, teachers, students, and community leaders, we have also benefited from observing and speaking with some of the brightest minds in the Quality movement. Here again, the list is too long to detail, but we give special recognition to David T. Kearns whose achievements in the education world and the Quality world are truly inspirational.

Initially, this was going to be a more straightforward, textbook-like guide to applying Quality principles to planning and designing of schoolhouses. However, by applying the very process that's described in this book to this book itself, we developed what we believe you, the customer, will find a more engaging, helpful and, we hope, inspiring resource. We thank Richard A. Segal Jr. for his significant and creative contributions to the content and style of this book. We thank Steve Kissing for enthusiastically managing the many details associated with creating, publishing and promoting this book. We also thank Mary Helmes for her impressive editing skills and Jim Folzenlogen for his graphic design expertise.

We thank our wives and our children whose Love has taught us the true meaning of Quality.

Gerald S. Hammond, FAIA
Stephen H. Schwandner, II